LUCINDA
O'SULLIVAN'S

Little Black Book of
Great Places to Stay

IRELAND

Enchanting Houses, Inns
Castles, Hotels and Spas

TSAR PRESS

This book is published by

TSAR PRESS

Post Office Box No. 9647
Glenageary, Co. Dublin.

www.lucindaosullivan.com
www.wheretostayinireland.com

Publishing Editor Brendan O'Sullivan
Written By Lucinda O'Sullivan

Regional Editor Margaret Browne
Maps and Mapping Joe Morris
Technical Support Ian O'Sullivan
Cover Ian O'Sullivan
Layout Susan Waine, Ashfield Press

Lucinda O'Sullivan has asserted her right to be identified
as author of this book

ISBN 0-9547256-1-1

Printed in Ireland by
Betaprint Ltd

A word from Lucinda

My *Little Black Book of Great Places to Stay* came about by virtue of all the letters and emails I have received over the years as Restaurant/Food Critic with the Sunday Independent saying, "You wrote about a place six months ago..." and asking me to do a book. Two years ago when I set out to write the First Edition, I had no idea that it would be such a resounding success. But thankfully it has been and so here now is the totally updated Second Edition, which includes fabulous new places for you to try out for yourselves.

As I have said before, Irish people are flying all over Europe, indeed the World, on great value tickets to see great value places. Grand, if that's what one wants. However, I have roasted beside pools in every country in Europe, I have drunk the Sangria and the Ouzo, sipped the Riesling and White Port, but I have never in any of these countries had the sheer unadulterated fun that you can have around Ireland, it's the people, the hilarity, the scenery, and I have kissed the tarmac at Dublin Airport every time I have come home to this infuriating little island of ours.

I have stayed in hundreds of houses and hotels and I have learned that the most expensive lauded establishment is not necessarily the greatest or most enjoyable place to stay for often they can be carried away with their own importance, be chilly, uncaring and offhand.

The Castles, Inns, Country and City Houses, Spas and special Hotels included in My Little Black Book are rich in their thinking and attitude towards the guest and the tourists. Some are lavish and luxurious, some are simple and sincere, some are creative and humorous, but here you can expect at all different levels, the finest of what Ireland has to offer by way of genuine hospitality, friendship, helpfulness and value for money in each category.

Don't forget to use the website www.lucindaosullivan.com through which you can contact me, share your experiences, and let me know if you have any wonderful discoveries. The website will be updated throughout the year.

Get out there and enjoy.

Lucinda

Ireland

I reland, perceived as the Emerald Isle, Land of the Shamrock, the Leprechaun, the Blarney Stone, Thatched and White Washed Cottages, and the attitude of "as God made time he made plenty of it" has changed dramatically in recent years. It is now a thriving progressive country holding its head high as a member of the European Union but City traffic is bumper to bumper from early morning as workers head for their places of employment to keep the wheels of progress turning. However, underneath all the hustle and bustle, people haven't changed all that much. They still like to meet and talk, share a story, have a laugh and generally enjoy life.

Sport is a major interest here. Our bloodstock industry, both racing and show jumping is respected world-wide. Irish golf courses are a match for any in the World and our golfers, of the standing of Padraig Harrington, Darren Clarke, Paul McGinley, regularly contest major competitions internationally. Rugby and soccer both have a solid following but the major football game is Gaelic football with interest reaching its climax at the end of September when the all Ireland Final between the two leading Counties is played. For visitors possibly the most fascinating sport is traditional hurling, which is probably the fastest field game in the world, requiring speed, fitness, physical strength, great skill and application.

The open countryside, from the pleasant valleys and rounded mountains of the East to the rugged features of the West, provide ample scope and pleasant diversity of scenery for the walker or cyclist. For the motorist there are limitless places of interest from ancient ruins, fine buildings and museums, breathtaking scenery and even a Fairy Tree on the Comeragh drive near Dungarvan. The gourmet is well catered for as each and every county provides some excellent Restaurants to please even the most demanding palate. Most pubs and bars provide good value lunches during the day and, in the evenings, many of them have traditional musicians and singers and, as we say in Ireland, the craic.

Most of all, apart from the sport, scenery, food, drink, craic, music the main attraction must be the people themselves, generally warm friendly and welcoming.

Ireland - you won't be disappointed.

EXPLANATION OF SYMBOLS

The symbols are a guide to facilities rather that a positive statement, and may change, so check important points when booking.

Working Farm

Children welcome, no age limits, but cots, high chairs etc are not necessarily available.

Credit Cards accepted – generally Visa/MC

T.V. in bedrooms

Swimming pool on premises

Parking

Wine or full License

Disabled Facilities – check level with establishment.

Internet access available

Pets welcome but may have to sleep in outbuilding or car. Check.

Pets accommodated in house.

Bikes on loan or for hire.

Tennis Court on premises

Helipad available

Golf Course on site

Contents

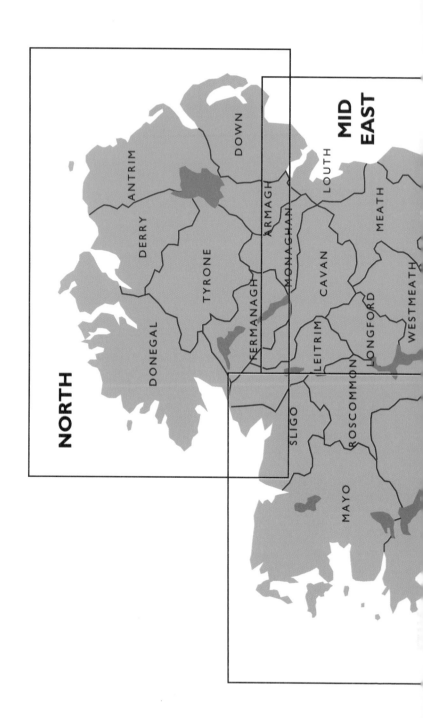

NORTH

MID
EAST

DONEGAL
DERRY
ANTRIM
TYRONE
DOWN
FERMANAGH
ARMAGH
MONAGHAN
CAVAN
LEITRIM
SLIGO
ROSCOMMON
LONGFORD
WESTMEATH
MEATH
LOUTH
MAYO

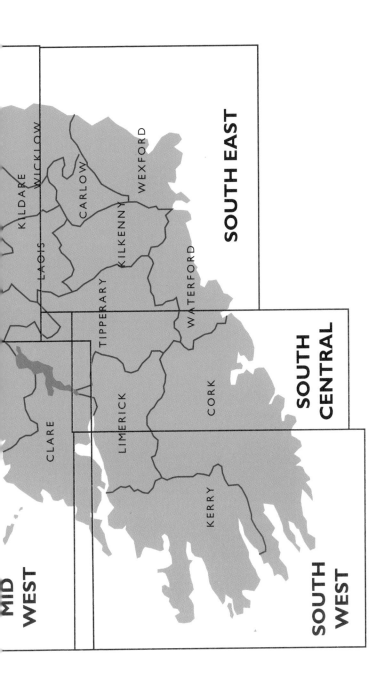

MID WEST

SOUTH EAST

SOUTH CENTRAL

SOUTH WEST

KILDARE

WICKLOW

LAOIS

CARLOW

WEXFORD

KILKENNY

TIPPERARY

WATERFORD

CLARE

LIMERICK

CORK

KERRY

North

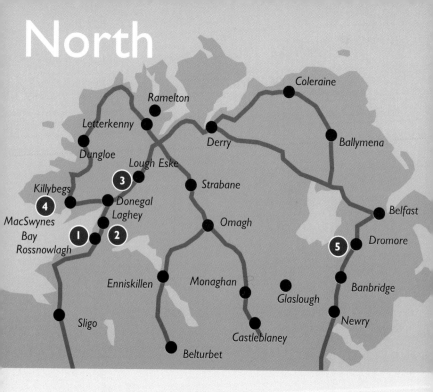

1. The Sandhouse Hotel & Marine Spa
2. Coxtown Manor
3. Harvey's Point Country Hotel
4. CastleMurray House Hotel
5. Clanmurry

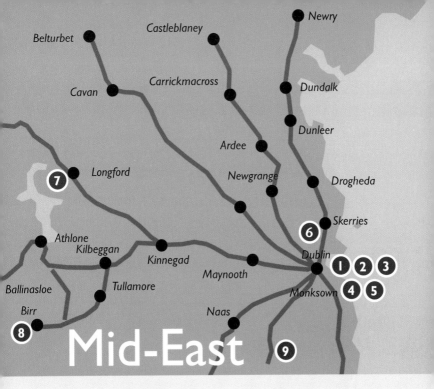

1. The Merrion Hotel
2. Conrad Hotel Dublin
3. Radisson SAS St. Helen's Hotel
4. Aberdeen Lodge
5. Drummond Mews
6. Redbank House & Restaurant
7. Viewmount House
8. The Stables Restaurant & Guesthouse
9. Barraderry Country House

South-East

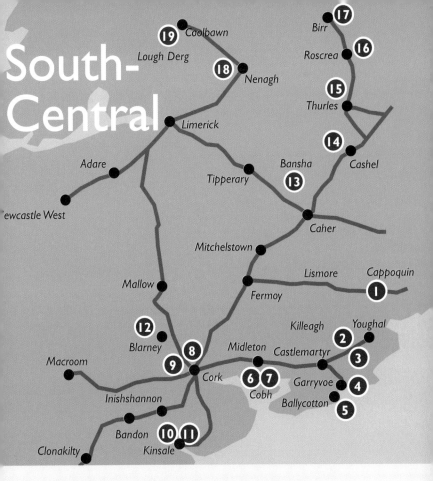

South-Central

1. Richmond House
2. Ballymakeigh Country House
3. Inchiquin House
4. Garryvoe Hotel
5. Bayview Hotel
6. Knockeven Country House
7. Watersedge Hotel
8. Hotel Isaac's Cork
9. Hayfield Manor
10. Blue Haven Hotel
11. Friar's Lodge
12. Ashlee Lodge
13. Bansha Castle
14. Bailey's of Cashel
15. Inch House & Restaurant
16. Monaincha House
17. The Stables Guesthouse & Restaurant
18. Ashley Park House
19. Coolbawn Quay

South-West

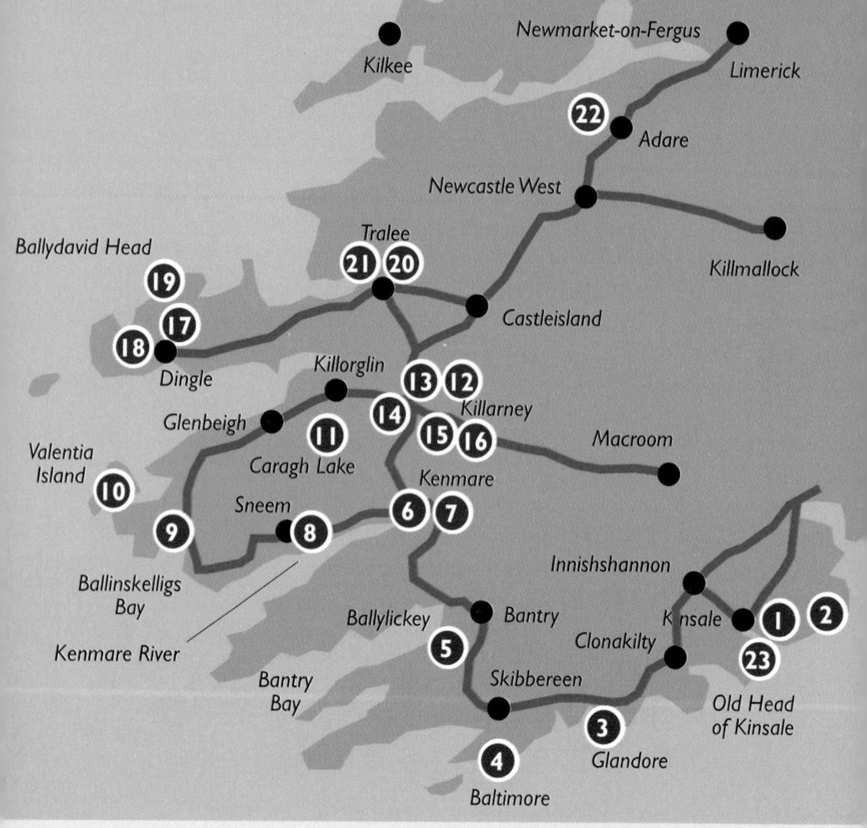

1. Blue Haven Hotel
2. Friar's Lodge
3. Kilfinnan Farmhouse
4. Baltimore Harbour Hotel
5. Seaview House Hotel
6. Muxnaw Lodge
7. Brook Lane Hotel
8. Great Southern Hotel Parknasilla
9. Butler Arms Hotel
10. Glanleam House & Estate
11. Carrig Country House & Restaurant
12. Great Southern Hotel Killarney
13. Aghadoe Heights Hotel & Spa
14. Loch Lein Country House Hotel
15. Cahernane House Hotel
16. Muckross Park Hotel & Spa
17. Heaton's Guesthouse
18. Castlewood House
19. Gorman's Clifftop House & Restaurant
20. Manor West Hotel
21. Meadowlands Hotel
22. Dunraven Arms Hotel
23. Shearwater

Mid-West

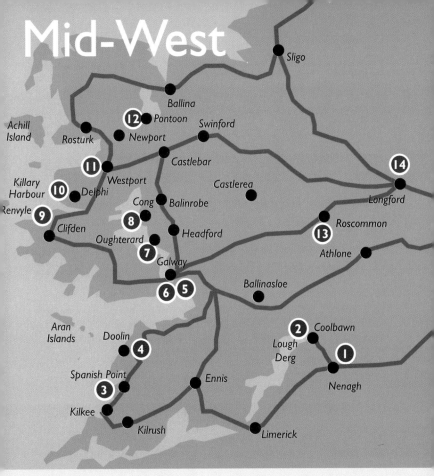

1	Ashley Park House	8	Ashford Castle
2	Coolbawn Quay Lakeshore Spa	9	Renvyle House Hotel
3	Admiralty Lodge	10	Delphi Mountain Resort & Spa
4	Ballyvara House	11	Ardmore House Hotel
5	Galway Radisson SAS Hotel	12	Pontoon Bridge Hotel
6	Great Southern Hotel	13	Gleeson's Townhouse
7	Ross Lake House Hotel	14	Viewmount House

County Carlow

Carlow is a low-rise busy midlands Town, on the River Barrow, and was an Anglo Norman stronghold at the edge of a very Gaelic county. Its present calm and serene atmosphere belies its turbulent past. At its heart is a beautiful classical Courthouse with the portico modelled on the Parthenon. Also worth seeing in Carlow is the controversial Regency Gothic Cathedral designed by Pugin. For those interested in Irish brew the Celtic Brewing Company, beside the Railway Station, is worth a tour. The beers brewed there are based on traditional Celtic recipes including a wheat beer, red ale and stout. Carlow has become a commuter town from Dublin and is developing rapidly, hence a plethora of new boutiques, restaurants, bars and cafés. Lennons and La Strada on Tullow Street are good buzzy spots with decent food. Teach Dolmen, also in Tullow Street, has impromptu traditional Irish music sessions. Two miles east of town on the R726 is Browneshill

Dolmen, possibly the largest Neolithic stone formation in Europe dating from 2500 BC. Seven miles south of Carlow on the N 9 is Leighlinbridge, the birthplace of Cardinal Cullen. Altamont Gardens near Tullow and Ballon are beautiful and attract many visitors. Borris, St. Mullins and the South Leinster Way are very popular with walkers and cyclists and are a great weekend destination. Carlow is mainly a farming county, which accounts for its easy going and generous atmosphere.

"You'll never plough a field by turning it over in your mind"
(Irish Proverb)

Ballyderrin House

M y happiest days as a child were spent at my Aunt's farm, The Grange, in Tullow. Hours were spent running up and down the avenue under dark overhanging trees, the best swing in the world was a branch of a big horse chestnut tree on the lawn, and days were spent "driving" a rusty old tractor skeleton. Tullow is a pretty town with a statue in the square erected to Fr. John Murphy who was "brutally put to death by the British". Uncle Tom took a visiting brother in law from England into town for a pint and, when the poor man saw the inscription on the statue, he thought he would never get back to the safety of Birmingham!

BALLYDERRIN HOUSE

Pamela and John Holligan's comfortable Ballyderrin House is on two acres of gardens surrounded by glorious countryside and woodland, against a backdrop of the Wicklow Mountains. Ballyderrin however is not just a place to rest one's weary head, for you are going to be under the care of a very fine cook. Pamela spent fifteen years in London working in top foodie establishments and is also Ballymaloe trained, so you are assured of beautifully prepared and presented food – organic where possible.

Having subsequently taught in Ballymaloe, Pamela set up her excellent Ballyderrin Cookery School. The School offers day, weekend and evening courses, which are held in fully equipped purpose built classrooms, under the tuition of highly skilled experts. So, you can combine a holiday, or a break, with acquiring knowledge. Pamela's cookery classes are fun too – I loved the idea of her BBQ evenings where, for a very reasonable charge, hubbie, partner or friends can come and join in when the food is cooked and make an evening out of the event. Aga Cookery weekends are very popular too, a great way to make new friends and enjoy the food together that you have cooked. Don't forget to visit their Café and Country Store and stock up with delicious jams, chutneys, breads, organic spices, herbs and wine.

Ballyderrin is ideally located, just ten minutes walk from the centre of the town, and from Mount Wolseley's Championship golf course if you fancy swinging a club. It is also an ideal fishing location along the River Slaney and they have facilities for pets.

I feel a trip to Tullow coming on …

Owners:	Pamela and John Holligan
Address:	Shillelagh Road,
	Tullow,
	Co. Carlow. .
Tel/Fax	059 9152742
No. Of Rooms	6
Price	
Double/Twin	€64/€70
Single	€45
Family	€70 + €27 for 3rd person or €5 B & B child under 5.
Dinner	Yes (must be booked in advance)
Open	All Year – Closed 24th, 25th, 26th December.
Credit Cards	All Major Cards
Directions.	From Tullow take the R725 towards Shillelagh
	Out of town 1/4 mile on left.
Email:	ballyderrinhouse@eircom.net
Web	www.lucindaosullivan.com/ballyderrin

Ballykealey Manor Hotel

Ted and Karen Egan's Ballykealey Manor Hotel is located at Ballon, a beautiful serene area with acres of greenery, forests and distant mountains. It is in the centre of a triangle between Carlow, Kilkenny and Enniscorthy, making it an ideal base from which to work outwards or just relax locally.   I was very interested when I heard Ted and Karen had taken over Ballykealey Manor as I had previously reviewed a restaurant owned by them and I knew that whatever this young couple took on they would do well – and they did.

Ballykealey Manor is a fabulously picturesque house with wonderfully outrageous Tudoresque cum Gothic features - and photo opportunities – you can't fail to be enchanted.   The house was built around 1830 by the well-known architect Thomas A Cobden for John James Lecky and his bride Sara Lucia Smith, and paid for by her generous dowry. Those were the days when what was hers became his on marriage! It was the time of the old Carlovian landed gentry, and the house remained in the Lecky family until the 1950's when Lieutenant Colonel Rupert

Beauchamp Lecky got into financial difficulties, disappeared and was never heard of again! However, the family motto is Semper Paratus Virtus Post Funera Vivit – Always Prepared, Virtue Endures beyond the Grave.

Set on seven rolling acres of landscaped lawns and wooded walks; there is a wonderful feeling of calm as you go up the drive and past the paddocks. The interior has the most amazing plasterwork, moulded cornices, architraves, wood panelling, and 10 ft solid oak dividing doors. You can crash out in the fabulous large opulent bedrooms filled

with splendid antiques or take yourself down to the very comfortable John Rupert's Bar for a jorum. In addition deluxe bedrooms have four-poster beds and spa baths in sunken level bathrooms – oh bliss.

Ted and Karen not only pamper you in the lap of luxury but their wonderful kitchen team produce the most sublime food. You might be feasting on seabass with pan-fried green bananas, glazed scallops and coconut chilli cream sauce or magret de canard with foie gras roulade, followed maybe by canon of lamb with kumquat jam and sweet roast shallots, or turbot, or Wicklow venison... So forget the diet, loosen the belt, and just enjoy Ballykealey's food and comfort.

Owners:	Ted and Karen Egan
Address:	Ballon,
	Co. Carlow.
Tel/Fax	059 9159288/059 915 9297
No. Of Rooms	12
Price	
Double/Twin	€150/€190
Single	€ 90
Family	€190
Dinner	Yes – Restaurant and Bar Food
Open	All Year – Closed 24th 25th 26th December
Credit Cards	Visa MC Laser
Directions.	15 km from Carlow Town on the Wexford Road – N80
Email:	ballykealeymanor@eircom.net
Web:	www.lucindaosullivan.com/ballykealeymanor

Barrowville Townhouse

Randal and Marie Dempsey's beautiful Barrowville Townhouse is a gracious and charming oasis in an otherwise mediocre world of B. & B's in Carlow Town. The house is magnificently furnished and, when you arrive on their doorstep on the Kilkenny Road, you will know with full and certain delight that you have made the right choice. Randal has an artistic eye and cannot resist a fine painting or good sculpture, whilst Marie is delightfully warm and friendly, bustling around ensuring you have every comfort. We were only too thrilled to sit at the garden table with a cool drink before setting off to review a Restaurant - it certainly put us in good humour anyway. I have stayed in different rooms in the house, all wonderfully comfortable, but one in particular is quite splendid running from back to front. Breakfast is served each morning in the prettiest raised conservatory off the Drawingroom, and is a spectacular feast in itself. Everything that you could possibly think of is available from fresh raspberries, loganberries, mueslies, juices, dried fruits, fresh fruits, smoked salmon plates, cheeses, cold meats, and then we get down to the hot food. Breads and croissants, all freshly baked by Marie, will be in silver breadbaskets and your boiled egg will come with silver eggcup

and spoon! Piping hot tea is in silver teapots and the crispest white linen cloths with napkins will be on the tables. I would drive this minute to Carlow for Marie Dempsey's poached eggs on potato cakes, complete with chives and slivers of mushroom. I tried to emulate them but failed miserably. This is a super house and perfect too for exploring Kilkenny and you can then return to the peace of Barrowville. There are lots of new Restaurants now in Carlow within walking distance. Children over 12 welcome.

Owners:	Randal and Marie Dempsey
Address:	Kilkenny Road, Carlow, Co. Carlow.
Tel/Fax	059 9143324/059 9141953
No. Of Rooms	7
Price	
Double/Twin	€90 - €99
Single	€55 - €65
Family	€125 (3 people)
Dinner	No
Open	All Year
Credit Cards	Visa MC Amex
Directions.	On right hand side heading south out of Carlow town on N9
Email:	barrowvilletownhouse@eircom.net
Web:	www.lucindaosullivan.com/barrowvillehouse

County Clare

County Clare is bordered by Galway to the north – the Atlantic to the west and the River Shannon on the east and south. Renowned as a stronghold of traditional music, it also offers many other attractions to the visitor. The Burren is a stark expanse of moonlike grey limestone and shale which is home to the most extraordinary flora and fauna and is a must visit. Kilkee is a seaside resort popular with families and scuba divers and has plenty of restaurants and pubs. Lahinch with its fabulous broad beach attracts surfers and boasts a magnificent golf course. The Cliffs of Moher attract a number of visitors as does the town of Doolin, four miles from the Cliffs. Doolin is for many the music centre of the west and you are sure to find some kind of merriment in one of the town's pubs (O'Connor's, McCann's and McDermott's). If you are unmarried and visit Lisdoonvarna in the month of September you may well find yourself "Spoken For" before you leave, for the town is famous for its month long Matchmaking Festival which comes after the Harvest has been saved.

Wedlock – "the deep, deep peace of the double bed
after the hurly burly of the chaise longue"
(Mrs. Patrick Campbell)

Admiralty Lodge

As a Canadian friend said to me, the remote rugged beauty of Clare is the Real Ireland, its what visitors want to see, and what many of us want to escape to. Out to the very west of County Clare is Spanish Point, with its enormous white crested waves, azure blue seas, crystal clear blue skies, its absolutely unspoilt magnificence is virtually unmatched. Having been to the Burren and the Cliffs of Moher, we were cruising down the coast road when we spotted a very new and interesting looking white building with Irish and American flags flying.

Admiralty Lodge had only opened the previous week. We were lucky because Pat O'Malley's new luxury 4 Star Country House is the best thing to have happened in centuries in County Clare. First thing I noticed was the large purple modern chaise longue in the hall. Then I looked into a beautiful anti-room, and on to the even more magnificent diningroom with grand piano in front of French Doors to the garden. I think this is probably the most beautiful diningroom in the country. The high, barrel shaped, white panelled ceiling holds three crystal chandeliers, which shimmer in the large over mantels at each end of the room. One wall is similarly panelled half way up and then dressed with sophisticated floral fabric whilst the other is red brick.

Well, you can't eat the décor, I can hear you say, but the food too is divine and not overpriced for its elegant simplicity and surroundings. This is a serious kitchen producing contemporary classical cuisine. Dinner might include Seared Scallops with an avocado mousse or a simply described Quail and new potato salad belying not so simple Ballotine of breast meat, drizzled with a fine frothy reduction, and the quail's leg perched on a baby new potato with a balsamic reduction. You might follow this up with perfectly pink trefoiled rump of lamb on

sweet potato with caramelised sweetbreads – and you'll die for the desserts.

Bedrooms are spacious, beautifully furnished, with king-size four-poster beds, Armoires, Chinoiserie wallpaper, and flat screen LCD televisions. I could hide in one of those rooms for a week and then sneak out to a local Seisun for the craic. Marbled bathrooms have power showers designed to either kill the hangover or administer an in-shower exfoliation.

Admiralty Lodge is perfect for golfers, for lovers, for foodies, take the helicopter or the batmobile and go now.

Owner:	Pat O'Malley	
Address:	Spanish Point, Co. Clare.	
Tel/Fax	065 7085007/065 7085030	
No.of Rooms	12	
Prices		
Double/Twin	€160 - €230	
Single	€125 - €165	
Dinner	Yes – Piano Room Diningroom	
Open	All Year	
Credit Cards	Visa MC Amex Laser	
Directions	From Ennis (Clare's main Town) take the Lahinch/Milltown Malbay Road. In Milltown take the Spanish Point Road and Follow signposts to Admiralty Lodge.	
Email:	info@admiralty.ie	
Web:	www.lucindaosullivan.com/admiralty	

Ballyvara House

Doolin is a pretty and popular village, in a dramatic setting, just four miles north of the Cliffs of Moher, close to the Burren, and ten minutes from Lahinch if you are a golfer! Also a take off point for the Aran Islands, it makes an ideal place in which to base oneself. Visit the sights during the day and enjoy the pubs and seisiuns at night. You want somewhere nice to stay that is where the new Ballyvara House comes in to play.

Ballyvara was once a charming farm cottage which John Flanagan inherited and which he turned into an approved B & B. However, John, a joiner and builder, took the idea much further and, retaining the stone and timber of the old cottage, has transformed the place into the spanking new Guest House it is today. Bedrooms are large and all have queen beds, spa or Jacuzzi baths, some even have balconies with stunning views. There are a couple of suites complete with large lounge and big T.V, mini-bar, and safe, so you don't have to carry around your valuables while sightseeing.

Located on 20 acres, there is a pretty courtyard garden but also plenty of room to romp around and children will love to go out and visit the donkey duo, Shetland and Welsh ponies, and the dogs. Ballyvara is a fun place with a little residents' bar where you can meet other visitors, have a drink and a bit of craic, and not worry about having to drive home. Excellent reasonably priced food

includes crab claws; Burren smoked salmon roulade or maybe a delicious home-made Italian style sausage with roasted peppers, buffalo mozzarella cheese, roasted garlic on a polenta cake. Follow up then with the fish dish of the evening or Barbary duck breast or steak. They always do a vegetarian dish and they have an extensive wine list. Breakfasts are brilliant – you can have the Full Irish or the Empty Irish and that, in case you didn't know, is eggs, bacon and tomato, without the sausage, pudding and beans! They also do delicious omelettes and luscious pancakes with syrup... If you so desire, instead of making a breakfast deadline...you can even have your breakfast in bed...most unusual for a Guest House.

John and Becky are welcoming hosts – you will be glad you discovered Ballyvara – I was.

					NET	P

Owners:	John Flanagan
Address:	Ballyvara, Doolin, Co. Clare.
Tel/Fax	065 7074467/065 7074868
No. Of Rooms	11
Price	
Suite	€110/€300
Double/Twin	€70/€200
Family	€35/€75 per person sharing
Dinner	Yes
Open	All Year – Closed 22-28 December
Credit Cards	Visa MC Amex Laser
Directions.	Once in Doolin village - from Roadford take the first Left after Cullinan's Restaurant (on right); Ballyvara is half mile up hill on left.
Email:	bvara@iol.ie
Web:	www.lucindaosullivan.com/ballyvarahouse

County Cork

Known as the Rebel County, for past deeds and the fact that Michael Collins was a native, Cork is the largest county in Ireland. An area of lush fertile farming land, and of fabulously indented coastline, it is also site of Ireland's second City. On the eastern side of the county there is the impressive little fishing port of Ballycotton. Close by is Shanagarry Pottery which is well worth a visit. Further along the coast is the historic town of Cobh, the harbour from which thousands of Irish emigrants departed for the U.S. and Australia, and was the last port of call of the ill fated Titanic. Close by Cobh is Fota Wildlife Park and, not far away, is a spot close to the heart of most Irish men – Midleton – the home of Jameson's Irish whiskey. Travel further west and visit Blarney Castle where you can kiss the famed Blarney Stone, said to endow one with the gift of the gab. Kinsale with its impressive Forts, narrow streets, and yachting marina is a picturesque town, and known as the gourmet capital of Ireland. Moving on west through Clonakilty you come to Rosscarbery, with its lovely Continental type village square, but swing left off the main road and wend your way to magnificent Glandore. Stop, take a seat by the wall, overlooking the water and have lunch. Take it easy and enjoy the peace. Further West is the nautically inclined very popular Baltimore. Travel on to Bantry Town which overlooks the famous bay of the same name and you can visit magnificent Bantry House, home of many art treasures. Move on then to the lushness and splendour of Ballylicky and Glengarriff, the last stop before entering the Kingdom of Kerry. And what about Cork City you might ask, for we Dubliners know that Cork is the "real" capital of Ireland. It is a major port on the estuary of the River Lee and this both lively and relaxed City is one of the most pleasurable urban areas in Ireland and is the south's self proclaimed cultural capital. This fantastic county with its rich pastoral land and its rugged coastline of beautiful bays and inlets has many places of historic and cultural interest and the natives are very friendly.

"Culture is roughly anything we do and monkeys don't"
(Lord Raglan)

Ashlee Lodge

Ashlee Lodge need never kiss the Blarney Stone, for it more than speaks for itself! It is one of a new breed of small distinctive private hotels and Guest Houses around Ireland offering the comforts and services of top hotels in a very personal way.

We were not in Blarney to kiss the legendary stone but on the way to Kerry when we spotted Ashlee Lodge which Anne and John O'Leary, had custom built to provide four suites and six large executive rooms, with wide screen TV's, C.D unit, modem access, Jacuzzi bath, an outdoor Canadian hot-tub, sauna, and an Honour Bar in the drawing-room.

What we didn't expect, when we swung into the car park by the meticulously kept little oriental garden, was the most delicious food on offer, for residents, served in their lovely modern conservatory restaurant, to which we were alerted by enticing aromas from the kitchen. You might be feasting on succulent braised shank of lamb or organic pan-fried chicken supreme on a bed of egg yellow fresh Tagliatelle as I was but, whatever you choose, it will be spot on, beautifully cooked, and puddings are divine. Starters are also available as mains so, if you just wanted a glass of wine and a plate of oak smoked West Cork salmon with pickled cucumber, capers, and red onion you could have it, or maybe vegetarian samosas, half shelled garlic mussels, or divine St. Tola goat's cheese with redcurrant and plum compote. Anne's breads are absolutely gorgeous and her salads wonderful – cashew nuts, stuffed olives,

garlic croutons, strawberries, raspberries, blueberries, grapes, pine nuts....

After you have slept that lot off you can stagger up to the breakfast buffet – strawberries, raspberries, blueberries, a myriad of cereals, cheeses, smoked salmon, cinnamon bagels with melted cheese, chunks of honey comb on your table.... not to mention eggs and the Full Irish.

Ashlee Lodge is also a Golfer's paradise. They will arrange your tee times and their courtesy coach will bring you to any of the 20 Golf Courses within 30 minutes drive. They will also meet you at the Airport.

Anne and John are the sort of people that we need in Irish tourism – they cosset you - Ashlee is a real cracker – don't be cynical - kiss the Blarney stone as well ... and its just down the road from Cork City.

Owners:	John & Anne O'Leary
Address:	Tower, Blarney, Co. Cork.
Tel/Fax	021 4385346/021 4385726
No. Of Rooms	10
Price	
Master Suite	€200
Garden Suite	€160
Double/Twin	€140
Single	€95
Family	Under 12's – 25% discount sharing with 2 adults
Dinner	Yes
Open	10th January to 20th December
Credit Cards	Visa MC Amex Diners Laser
Directions.	Located on R617 Blarney/ Killarney Road in Tower Village, 4 minutes from Blarney.
Email:	info@ashleelodge.com
Web:	www.lucindaosullivan.com/ashlee

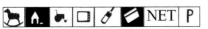

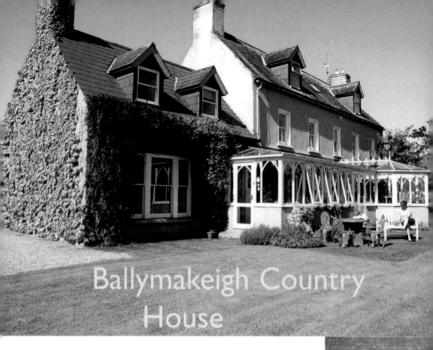

Ballymakeigh Country House

As if on cue, 200 glorious Friesian cows trundled from the fields, in what seemed like a never-ending line for milking, as we arrived at Ballymakeigh House. Margaret and Michael Browne's lovely 300-year-old Farmhouse has won every award in the book and continues to do so. Not just has the house won awards but Margaret, who is Cork's answer to Superwoman, has been Housewife of the Year, T.V. Chef and published her own best selling cookery book "Through My Kitchen Window". Ballymakeigh is a fun place because Margaret and Mike are absolutely irrepressible loving nothing more than a bit of hilarity. This is a very interesting old house which has calming bedrooms with, as Margaret might say herself, "bags of old fashioned comfort", and of course, perfectly fitted and kitted out en suite bathrooms. If you are feeling energetic, there is a hard tennis court, or you can walk the land, see the milking parlour, or merely sit down in the lovely big conservatory for the day with a glass in hand – nobody will bat an eyelid. Americans love to visit "real Irish" homes and this I can tell you is a "real Irish" home, but with everything running to perfection down to the ice machine. A spanking dinner is served in the lovely old world red diningroom. Breakfasts are hearty with fresh pressed apple juice, fruits and yoghurts, traditional grainy porridge with spices, cereals, kippers with thyme, and a super "Full Irish" including rashers, sausages, Clonakilty pudding tomatoes and eggs.

Preserves, of course, are homemade as are the breads - traditional Irish soda bread and leek and onion savoury scones are to die for. Mark my words, like me, you will go back again and again to Ballymakeigh.

Owners:	Michael and Margaret Browne
Address:	Killeagh, Co. Cork.
	Tel/Fax
	024 95184/024 95370
No. Of Rooms	6
Price	
Double/Twin	€110 - €120
Single	€75
Family	On request
Dinner	Yes
Open	All Year
Credit Cards	Visa MC Amex
Directions.	Located 1 mile off N25. 22 miles east of Cork City. Signposted in Killeagh village at Old Thatch Pub.
Email:	ballymakeigh@eircom.net
Web:	www.lucindaosullivan.com/ballymakeighhouse

Baltimore Harbour Hotel

altimore is a fishing village at the very south of Ireland, spectacularly located looking out to Roaringwater Bay and the Carbery Islands. It is about as far south and out into the water as you can get. A magnet for the "yachties", particularly in July and August during regatta time, so accommodation is at a premium. In Baltimore there is a Sailing Club, two Sailing Schools and two Diving Schools and water is the key word here. Whilst the "junior yachties" are learning the ropes, Mum and Dad can relax and enjoy the local amenities and facilities at The Baltimore Harbour Hotel. Ideally located overlooking the harbour, the Hotel has 64 lovely bedrooms, a 16m swimming pool, bubble pool, children's pool, as well as a sauna, steam room, and treatment rooms for massage and reflexology. I really loved the two and three bedroomed courtyard suites at the Hotel. These suites are not self catering but do have a spacious lounge/kitchen area with a kettle, fridge and microwave and some have balconies. We stayed with our two teenage sons and found the "suite" idea wonderful because when we wanted to socialize in the hotel they could stay behind and watch TV without just being confined to a bedroom. Food at the hotel's Clipper Restaurant is excellent using the best of local West Cork fresh produce and plenty of seafood – think Crab Claw Salad with Citrus dressing or Fresh Tuna Steak on a bed of squid ink Tagliatelle with tomato Herb Sauce. The staff are very friendly and obliging and will cater for all needs and they have a comprehensive children's menu. There are a number of interesting pubs and cafes in Baltimore and ferries leave each day to Cape Clear, which has incredible bird life, and for Sherkin Island which has two lovely sandy beaches. The hotel's

Chartroom Bar has music sessions in summer and at weekends or alternatively you might enjoy sitting in the local square with a cool drink watching the sun go down over the islands.   Paradise Regained.

Owners:	Charles Cullinane.
Address:	Baltimore, Co. Cork.
Tel/Fax	028 20361/028 20466
No. Of Rooms	64
Price	
Double/Twin	€150 (special rates available throughout year on request)
Single	€90
Family	€200 (2 Adults + 2 Children)
Dinner	Yes - Restaurant
Open	February – 21st December
Credit Cards	All Major Cards
Directions.	Signposted on the right on entry to Baltimore
Email:	info@baltimoreharbourhotel.ie
Web:	www.lucindaosullivan.com/baltimoreharbouthotel

Bayview Hotel

Ballycotton is a completely unspoiled Fishing Village in East Cork dating back to 1250 AD.   Not only is it completely unspoiled but it is also largely undiscovered save by those in the know, for people tend to dash on further west to the overblown more high profile villages. Once you turn down at Castlemartyr you whirl around the back roads amongst high hedges and fertile fields which are eons away from the modern world - and yet so near.   Ballycotton is an ideal base for visiting Cork, if you prefer to stay out of a City, or for taking a leisurely tour of Stephen Pearce's Pottery and for visiting Ballymaloe, and the Jameson Irish Whiskey Centre at Midleton, after which you might need to be careful on the Ballycotton Cliff Walk!!

BAYVIEW HOTEL BALLYCOTTON

I have had a problem for a number of years with Hotels and Restaurants, a problem which can spoil one's entire visit - namely - the "back room" and the "table beside the toilet door" respectively.   I have been offered a far from romantic attic in Paris, a box in London beside a lift shaft with pneumatic drills working in it, "no sea view" all over the place, a room over the rubbish exit in Palma, and even rooms with no view at all save the sidewall of the next building.   The Bayview Hotel in my eyes is just perfectly designed for all the rooms have magnificent sea views.   As you look out it feels more like a "visual tour" because you are just over the sheer drop onto the rocks, gazing out into infinity, broken only by the old world little quaint Ballycotton Harbour.   Not only does the newly revamped Bayview have 35 perfect rooms, a comfortable library style bar and lounge, it has excellent food provided by Head Chef, Ciaran Scully, who cooks up the best of French style food in The

Capricho Restaurant in this special little gourmet Hotel. Think prawns the size of your thumb and silky foie gras....... There are six golf courses within 30 minutes drive, as well as some of the best sea angling in Europe. Stephen Belton provides a 5 star service at the 4 star Bayview. Go and discover it for yourself.

Owners:	John & Carmel O'Brien
	Stephen Belton
	(General Manager)
Address:	Ballycotton, Co. Cork.
Tel/Fax	021 4646746/021 4646075
No. Of Rooms	35
Price	
Double/Twin	€160 - €198
Single	€112
Dinner	Yes
Open	Mid April to end October
Credit Cards	All Major Cards
Directions.	Located in Ballycotton Village
Email:	res@thebayviewhotel.com
Web:	www.lucindaosullivan.com/bayviewhotel

The Blue Haven Hotel

I was at the very first Kinsale Gourmet Festival in the mid 70's when it was a fledgling event but, like Topsy, it just growed and growed, along with it Kinsale's reputation worldwide on the foodie scene. A pivotal part of this foodie arena has always been the Blue Haven Hotel, which was run like a very tight ship and into which everybody seemed to report at some part of the day. We have had great nights there with people from all over the world in Kinsale for shark fishing, the food, sailing or just the fun of the whole place. In fact on one occasion we had such an hilarious stay it took us three days to leave! We got up each morning with the best of intentions but, we would meet someone we knew, and after a couple of "farewell" jars couldn't set off to drive to Dublin so, back we would have to go to Reception, and beg for our room, or any room!

Local guy, Ciaran Fitzgerald, is now at the helm of the Blue Haven and has spent the past two years revamping and restoring it into a very fine atmospheric and welcoming Boutique type Hotel. All of the very stylish bedrooms have had a major face lift to bring them in line with the requirements of today's discerning traveller - flat screen TV's, those really expensive beds, pillow menus, wild wood furniture, wireless broadband and spanking newly fitted bathrooms.

There is a new relaxed bistro restaurant now in situ called Blu with an outdoor deck and pre dinner drinks area. The food is modern, well executed and just what is wanted nowadays. You can think perhaps of lobster, scallops, or prawns, partnered with good Mediterranean vegetables, asparagus, artichokes, aubergines and followed by scrumptious puds. There is food all over the place at the Blue Haven for there is also the more informal dining option in the Bar, Conservatory and a deck area called The Fishmarket complete with outdoor heaters and an overhead canopy. Really good food is available all day so if you want to be at the hub in Kinsale – The Blue Haven is the place to be – you never know if you are lucky it might take you 3 days to check out!

 NET

Owners:	Ciaran Fitzgerald
Address:	Pearse Street, Kinsale, Co. Cork.
Tel/Fax	021 4772209/021 4774268
No. Of Rooms	17
Price	
Double/Twin	€160 - €220
Single	€75 - €130
Family	€160- €280
Dinner	Yes – Restaurant, Bar Food and Coffee Shop
Open	All Year
Credit Cards	Visa MC Amex Laser
Directions.	Follow signs for the South Link and the airport and you will join the R27. After passing Cork Airport, three miles further on at the Five-Mile-Bridge take the R600 to Kinsale Town.
Email:	info@bluehavenkinsale.com
Web	www.lucindaosullivan.com/bluehaven

Friar's Lodge

The first time I met Maureen Tierney we had arrived with two small boys in the car, hot, tired and ratty. Jack Charlton was the Irish Soccer Team Manager, it was "Ole Ole Year"- 1990 when Ireland took the summer off to support the Irish Team in the World Cup. We were renting a self-catering house from her. She strolled up the street smiling and cool, immediately lowering our stress levels – nothing seemed to faze her and nothing was a problem.

Maureen Tierney has always been ahead of the game. In recent years, various luxury B & Bs and Guesthouses have come on stream in Kinsale and they may well be very excellent but some are also very expensive, catering for wealthy golfers coming to play at the Old Head. Maureen said to herself "what about providing luxury accommodation but at reasonable prices" and Friar's Lodge was born.

In the centre of town, nothing is lacking for Maureen's specifications were meticulous for her new venture which is proving a real winner. Friar's Lodge is built over and around a central archway, leading to ample private parking and three self-catering houses. The rooms and suites are like good hotel rooms, spacious, with all creature comforts, turn down service, choccies on your pillow – a pillow menu – telephone, TV, DVD, radio, internet connection, safe, ironing centre, mini bar available, and of course an elevator. You can also bring your pet – but do enquire first cos that doesn't include elephants or alligators!

There are lovely relaxing lounge areas where you can sit and chat

with other guests or read the magazines. Maureen and her staff provide that extra 4 Star Service and will make any reservations you wish or arrange tee times – there is also a drying room for golfers. There is a compact wine menu available to residents and complimentary sherry sits in the decanter just waiting for you to have that aperitif before you toddle out to one of the many famous Kinsale restaurants. Breakfasts are delicious – help yourself to the cereals, fruits, and juices and then have a hot breakfast. "Would you like some fish," said Maureen, "we just run down to the local fish shop – which is particularly good – and bring it in fresh........."

Nothing is ever too much trouble for Maureen Tierney – she is still smiling and unflappable – outstanding – loves horses and is definitely in the winner's enclosure.

Owners:	Maureen Tierney
Address:	Friar's Street, Kinsale, Co. Cork.
Tel/Fax:	021 4777384/021 4774363
No. Of Rooms:	18
Price:	
Suite/Family:	€140 Children under 5 free.
Double/Twin:	€120
Single	€80
Dinner	No – Kinsale is awash with restaurants.
Open	All Year – Closed 22nd – 28th December.
Credit Cards	Visa MC Amex Laser
Directions:	Follow signs for the South Link and the airport and you will join the R27. After passing Cork Airport, three miles further on at the Five-Mile-Bridge take the R600 to Kinsale Town.
Email:	mtierney@indigo.ie
Web:	www.lucindaosullivan.com/friarslodge

NET P

Garryvoe Hotel

Garryvoe in East Cork is to scores of Corkonians what Skerries is to Dubliners, and maybe what Long Island was to New Yorkers – where the childhood holidays were spent. Long innocent days on the beach, simple fun in rented summer houses or caravans, sand in the banana sandwiches and romps through the rough grass with Fido, beach balls, rounders and windbreakers, it was not in any way sophisticated. Fond memories.

For Irish people along with those memories of Skerries, Garryvoe, and sand filled sandwiches, is the taste of those wonderful Dublin Bay Prawns - which we took for granted – great big bruisers that our parents used to buy straight from the Fishing boats, pop in the boiling water for a flash and eat with salt and mayonnaise. They are nearly a thing of the past on Irish menus now, replaced by every old excuse of a prawn from distant shores, but I can let you in on a secret - at the Garryvoe Hotel you will also find them on the menu in bucket loads - Prawn Cocktail - the real thing - Prawns with Garlic Butter - the real thing - Prawn Scampi - the real thing - Prawns Mornay - you haven't seen that in a while have you?

The Garryvoe Hotel was for many years a solid country hotel but has been transformed into a magnificent new establishment with superb bedrooms and suites overlooking the beach. It has a swish new diningroom complete with twinkling ceiling, and smart new bar. We were in a glorious Junior Suite with a wonderful high cathedral ceiling - I could have stayed in that room for a week without leaving it – and lived on room service. It was so cool and calming with a giant sized bed, beautiful big brown sofas, clear white walls, blue curtains and a view of the sea that seemed never ending. We left the balcony doors open all night to hear the lapping of the waves – it was just bliss.

There is a generosity of spirit too in The Garryvoe both with Stephen Belton, the General Manager, and John and Carmel O'Brien who also own the Bayview Hotel in Ballycotton. Garryvoe is just beside Ballymaloe and Shannagarry and is a superb place to stay.

Owners:	John & Carmel O'Brien
	Stephen Belton,
	General Manager.
Address:	Garryvoe, Castlemartyr,
	East Cork.
Tel/Fax	021 4646718/021 464 6824
No. Of Rooms	48
Price	
Double/Twin	€150
Single	€100
Family	€175
Dinner	Yes - Restaurant
Open	All Year
Credit Cards	Visa MC Amex Diners Laser
Directions.	In the heart of Garryvoe
	village facing the beach
Email:	res@garryvoehotel.com
Web:	
www.lucindaosullivan.com/garryvoe	

NET H P

45

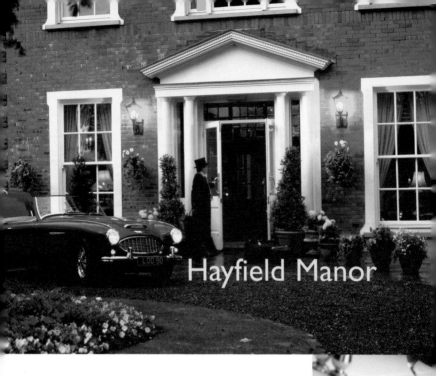

Hayfield Manor

"Thelma and Louise" said the General Manager, of the 5 Star Hayfield Manor Hotel welcoming and helping the windblown disheveled pair scramble out of the low open topped car with their bags.   It is not very often that the General Manager of any Hotel is at the door to greet one – they are usually hiding away in their Offices leaving the front of house stuff to their minions.   I must say it was very impressive and this hands on approach clearly results in a very high standard of performance all round. Hayfield Manor, a member of the Small Luxury Hotels of the World, is where the Legal fraternity rest their briefs when in Cork – and believe me they like their comforts.   A red bricked neo-Georgian building set in two acres of ground with mature trees and surrounded by a 15-foot wall. Located beside the University it has a magnificent new Spa, along with shimmering Pool and Beauty Salon just for residents' use.   The first impression is "oh, its so pretty" - like a Connecticut Mansion in an American movie – everything perfect with a lovely old picturesque tree right outside the front door, topiary planters, carriage lights, and a liveried doorman.   The bedrooms are beautifully draped and lavishly furnished and I got to sleep in the suite used by Pierce Brosnan and his wife just after they departed! I felt like I never wanted to leave it. This is

where anyone who is anyone stays when they come to Cork. There is an air of being cushioned away from the real world at Hayfield and, although it is 5 star, it is absolutely unpretentious. Fabulous food is served in The Manor Room Restaurant Marble Terrine of Foie Gras layered with poached figs, compote of figs, dried pears; Filet Mignon of Dutch Veal, Truffle Risotto, roasted asparagus with artichoke with truffle sauce whilst in the lovely new light and airy conservatory style fashionable Perrot's Restaurant there is a superb selection of modern food at very reasonable prices. Hayfield, a wonderful luxurious oasis in Cork, only a mile from Patrick Street and is the perfect place for business or pleasure. Enquire too about their special breaks. I just want to live permanently in the picture postcard world of Hayfield Manor.

Owners:	Joe and Margaret Scally
Address:	Hayfield Manor, Perrott Avenue, College Road, Cork.
Tel/Fax	021 4845900/0214316839
No. Of Rooms	88
Price	
Suites	From €475
Double/Twin	€380
Single	€380
Dinner	Yes – 2 Restaurants
Open	All Year
Credit Cards	Visa MC Amex Diners Laser
Directions	Signed off College Road

Email: enquiries@hayfieldmanor.ie
Web: www.lucindaosullivan.com/hayfieldmanor

Hotel Isaacs

The idea for Hotel Isaacs was inspired. A vast, red bricked, Victorian landmark building on Cork's MacCurtain Street, used by Nat Ross Removals, was converted into Hotel Isaacs, offering great value accommodation in excellent surroundings.

The Hotel is an oasis of calm, entered through a cobblestone archway, with the very stylish lobby having beautiful original paintings. Hotel Isaacs always had a reputation for meticulous housekeeping but has undergone a major refurbishment and the bedrooms, which are very modern, bright, airy and comfortable, have had a total revamp. Apart from all the standard comforts, they are ideally suited for the technophile – modems, safes, minibars, transcontinental built in adaptors, ISDN phone line, air conditioning, trouser press, iron and ironing boards. The location is brilliant for Hotel Isaacs is surrounded by restaurants, clubs, pubs, boutiques and antique and décor shops.

Greene's the Hotel's own in-house Brasserie style restaurant is under the baton of French chef, Frederic Deformeau. It overlooks a floodlit cascading feature waterfall, so you are ideally placed for a fun gourmet weekend. Park the car, have a drink in the bar and forget about driving – or you can come by train – the station is just up the street. The food is excellent, and you can think perhaps of lovely fresh timbale of crab with avocado, lemon and chive mayonnaise topped with toasted brioche or French "Chavignol" goats cheese stuffed with semi-dried tomato and black olives, wrapped in Parma Ham and served on spicy red onion bruschetta drizzled with balsamic and olive oil. One of my favourite dishes there is a parcel of Savoy Cabbage filled with an excellent duck confit and vegetable brunoise served on spicy Puy lentils with a rich deep red wine jus. That always makes my trip to Greene's worthwhile – a little bit of rustic France in the Rebel County. Mains include excellent shellfish or smoked fish antipasti, shank of lamb on confit roast potatoes or pink rack of lamb.

There are also 11 two and three bedroom apartments adjacent to the hotel, which have also been revamped, and are very popular with small groups, families and business people who like a bit more space and freedom. At Hotel Isaacs you are at the heart of Cork.

Owners:	Paula Lynch (General Manager)	
Address:	48 MacCurtain Street, Cork.	
Tel/Fax	021 4500011/021 4506355	
No. Of Rooms	47	
Price		
Double/Twin	€110 - €260	
Single	€80 - €155	
Family	€140 - €220 (2 Bed Apartment)	
Dinner	Yes - Restaurant	
Open	All Year -- except 24/25/26 December	
Credit Cards	All Major Cards	
Directions.	From Patrick Street follow directions to Cork Railway Station. Hotel on left in one-way traffic system. Email: cork@isaacs.ie Web: www.lucindaosullivan. com/hotelisaacs	

Inchiquin House

At some stage in our lives we all have a vision of discovering a gorgeous house tucked away in the countryside, as well furnished and as comfortable as our own home, and being able to play house there for a week or two without any of the responsibilities. It is not easy but I have found such a precious gem, Inchiquin House. Michael and Margaret Browne are perfectionists, so the house is lovingly restored. Big and spacious, this Victorian five bedroomed house has beds that are only equalled in comfort with the beds in their other establishment, the nearby Ballymakeigh House. My favourite bedroom is on the ground floor with French doors opening out on to the gardens. The house has four bathrooms and a very functional and pleasant kitchen facing west. The kitchen is the focal point of the house by day and the large sittingroom with open fire is there to while away the night in comfort. There is a very attractive dining area which would be perfect for

entertaining friends and family or, alternatively, you can also book yourself into Ballymakeigh House for dinner. Expect a welcome pack of Ballymakeigh preserves and bread on arrival. Inchiquin House is conveniently located at the end of a tree lined avenue off the N25, twenty miles east of Cork City and two miles from Youghal and is perfect too for visiting Ballymaloe, Midleton, Lismore, and all the surrounding areas.

Owners:	Michael and Margaret Browne
Address:	Killeagh, Co. Cork.
Tel/Fax	024 95184/024 95370
No. Of Rooms	5
Price	€500 - €800 per week self catering.
Dinner	Available at Ballymakeigh House
Open	All Year
Credit Cards	Visa MC
Directions.	Ring for directions
Email:	Ballymakeigh@eircom.net
Web:	www.lucindaosullivan.com/inchiquin

Kilfinnan Farmhouse

Along the south west coastline of West Cork which is a myriad of little bays and creeks, sandy coves, tidal loughs and magical ocean sprays is Glandore, a glorious coastal tiny village comprising a little harbour, a couple of pubs, a small hotel, and a Restaurant high on the hill. So enticing is Glandore that it surely got separated from its Italian mother during the ice age landing instead on Irish shores to bring a little continental glamour. It is spectacularly beautiful and a magnet for wealthy Dublin and Cork people. Glandore is relatively undiscovered by Tourists who "don't turn down" but keep going on the main road through Leap (pronounced Lep) like the clappers heading further West not realizing that the whole point of West Cork and Kerry is to amble and socialise, not race through it. They don't know what they are missing. The two pubs that pretty well make up Glandore have tables by a low wall on this natural "terrace" but if you don't get there early in the summertime you have had it. The whole point about Glandore is not just to admire the view but to "people watch". You sit there, with your friends, enjoying pretty sandwiches from "Hayes Bar" for as long as possible, observing the top of the range cars and their drivers cruise slowly through..........

Accommodation in Glandore is at a premium but just an Irish mile away, high up overlooking Glandore Harbour, is Margaret Mehigan's lovely family run Kilfinnan Farmhouse which, apart from being lovely, offers super, very reasonably priced, accommodation. The sweet old ivy clad house has four en suite bedrooms with really comfortable beds, crisp bedlinen and pretty views, some overlooking the old world garden. You are likely to meet Margaret's sister in law, Ann, bringing the cows in for milking as you arrive whilst Margaret, meantime,

envelopes you in the warmth of her welcome. Don't expect foil-covered butters and shop bought marmalade at Kilfinnan. Everything is beautifully presented in pretty dishes and the milk, eggs, meat, fruit and vegetables are freshly produced on the farm so you can only benefit. Kilfinnan is surrounded by pretty little beaches which for the most part of the year are virtually unoccupied. There are all sorts of water based activities nearby – water-skiing, sailing, and diving down to look at all the wrecks which came a cropper. The stunningly impressive Bronze Age Drombeg stone circle, made up of a formation of seventeen stones, is just across the fields leading down to the water. Nearby there is also a fulacht fiadh, which is an ancient cooking site where troughs of water would have been heated by hot stones thrown into them from a fire. Kilfinnan Farm is a real find in a real Ireland – don't tell anyone.

Owner:	Margaret Mehigan
Address:	Kilfinnan Farm, Glandore, Co. Cork.
Tel/Fax	028 33233
No. Of Rooms	4
Price	
Double	€80
Twin	€80
Single	€50
Family	Negotiable (Children under 4 free. Discount under 14's)
Dinner	High Tea available
Open	All Year
Credit Cards	No
Directions.	Take R597 to Glandore. Watch for signpost to left for house.
Email:	kilfinnanfarm@eircom.net
Web:	www.lucindaosullivan.com/kilfinnanfarm

Knockeven House

Cobh, as most people know, was the final departure point of the ill-fated Titanic Liner on its maiden voyage to New York in 1912. Not only is it a nostalgic town for that reason but, for thousands of Irish people, Cobh (formerly known as Queenstown) was the last image of Ireland as they emigrated to America with many never returning to their native land.. It is quite a spectacular image to retain in one's memory for, sailing out of Cobh Harbour, looking back at the houses stacked up the hill under the spire of the elaborate almost fairy tale neo Gothic, Pugin designed, Cathedral is particularly beautiful.

Thousands of people visit Cobh each year to retrace the footsteps of their ancestors and to visit the wonderful Cobh Heritage Centre. Strangely enough I have to confess that I did not discover Knockeven House myself - although I am often in that area – I heard about it from somebody living in New York who contacted me to tell me how wonderful it was ... and it is.

I am pathologically fussy about where I stay because it can make such a difference to the enjoyment of one's entire holiday but believe me

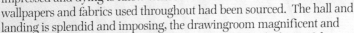

if you stay at John and Pam Mulhaire's beautiful home you will not only enjoy it you will be suitably impressed and enchanted all at once. Knockeven House was built in 1840 and the graciousness of the era is evident all over this splendid house. This has been Pam and John's home for twenty years but they have only recently totally and lavishly revamped the house with incredible style and taste and opened it up to guests. We were very impressed and dying to know where the beautiful wallpapers and fabrics used throughout had been sourced. The hall and landing is splendid and imposing, the drawingroom magnificent and gracious, whilst the beautiful

diningroom overlooks the conservatory. The oversized bedrooms are divine and Pam's kitchen is straight out of House & Garden. To add to all of this magnificence, Pam and John are delightful. Pam chatters away and John is a good man for amusing stories when he is not out minding his beautiful gardens.

Knockeven House offers superb glorious accommodation at a fraction of the cost of similar accommodation in a top Hotel and is perfect also for visiting Cork City as you are over the river on the little ferry in a few minutes and you can also whiz out on the South Ring to West Cork.

Owners:	John and Pam Mulhaire
Address:	Rushbrooke, Cobh, Co. Cork.
Tel/Fax	021 4811778/021 4811719
No. Of Rooms	4
Price	
Double/Twin	€100 - €120
Single	€65 - €75
Family	€150
Dinner	No
Open	1st February – 2nd January
Credit Cards	Visa MC
Directions.	From Cork. N25 in direction Rosslare Waterford. Take Cobh exit R624. Pass Fota Wildlife Park over the bridge. Turn left at The Great Island Garage. First right avenue to Knockeven House.
Email:	info@knockevenhouse.com
Web:	www.knockevenhouse.com

NET P

Sea View House Hotel

"**Y**es, we do breakfast in bed ... if necessary," said the wonderful Miss Kathleen O'Sullivan, Proprietress of the Sea View House Hotel at Ballylickey, in response to my timorous enquiry on the telephone the night before. We felt like two naughty schoolgirls – but yes, they did breakfast in bed all right and, as one would expect under Kathleen O'Sullivan's eagle eye, it arrived on the button of 8 a.m. and was just perfect. A new wing has recently been added to the Sea View House, along with a magnificent French classical style round "conservatory" to the dining room, and it is just a fab place to stay. All of the rooms are splendid with larger rooms being absolutely divine – some opening out to the gardens – beautifully furnished with antiques, French Armoires and headboards, wonderful paintings – each different and each special. We had arrived like two exhausted rats into the hall of the Sea View having driven in and out of every peninsula from Cork to Ballylickey. Make no mistake

this takes hours, but I don't feel I have had my fix of West Cork each Summer without doing it. Having showered and dickied ourselves up we went down the corridor past Kathleen O'Sullivan's "Command Centre". "You look very nice", she said to my companion – "go through that door there and you can have a drink". Having passed muster we went into a cocktail bar and armed ourselves with suitable Sherries and set down to peruse the menus. The food is excellent – think Sauté Lamb kidneys Madeira sauce, whisper light Scampi or avocado with real Dublin Bay Prawns, Rack of Lamb or lemon sole all perfectly produced and served. "Do we get both Puddings and Cheese?" asked a young Englishman sitting across from us with his wife. His eyes lighting up like a child's when given the affirmative answer. We all looked together at a Victor Meldrew look-alike who passed by us and the young man said "we feel very young" – "so do we", we chimed sharply" to this mere fresh faced youth. The Sea View House Hotel is brilliant – you will absolutely love it.

Owners:	Kathleen O'Sullivan
Address:	Ballylickey, Bantry, Co. Cork.
Tel/Fax	027 50073/027 51555
No. Of Rooms	25
Price	
Mini Suite	€175 - €200
Double/Twin	€140 - €165
Single	€95 - €105
Family	€175
Dinner	Yes
Open	Mid March to Mid November
Credit Cards	All Major Cards
Directions.	Located on main Bantry to Glengarriff road.
Email:	info@seaviewhousehotel.com
Web:	
www.lucindaosullivan.com/seaviewhousehotel	

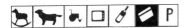

Shearwater

Without a doubt, Kinsale is on the itinerary of pretty well every tourist who comes to our shores, be they foodies or yachtties, or just plain wanting to visit this pretty town, which has achieved worldwide fame. We went on our honeymoon to Kinsale and have been up and down a few times every year since to this gorgeous romantic town with its narrow colourful streets and myriad of restaurants. There is always a buzz in Kinsale - be it winter or summer – in fact we like it even better out of season

Right on the marina, just beside Kinsale Yacht Club, is Shearwater, a new development of magnificent prime apartments and duplexes in what is probably the most stunning location in Ireland, never mind Kinsale, unrivalled and unprecedented.

Available for short term letting in Shearwater is a magnificent

duplex, which very comfortably sleeps up to 4 people. The steps up to the front entrance bring you into your own little world that is so modern and airy it has the feel and panache of a New York loft. The first floor has two bedrooms, a kingside bed in a spacious master bedroom with ensuite, beautifully furnished and draped. The second bedroom has twin beds and both have views of the Harbour.

Upstairs leads you to the most amazing enormous room with high cathedral ceiling, big picture window with view of the boats and out over the rooftops of Kinsale. Very stylishly furnished with a big hanging wall tapestry and eclectic Franco Chinese furnishings. The kitchen area is beautifully constructed and fitted with everything anyone could possibly want but then maybe you will be dining out in the dozens of restaurants for which Kinsale is famous.

Owners:	Mary O'Sullivan
Address:	Shearwater, Kinsale, Co. Cork.
Tel	01 2800419
No. Of Rooms	Sleeps 4
Price	From €695 per week
Dinner	Self Catering Duplex
Open	All Year
Credit Cards	All Major Cards
Directions.	On Marina
Email:	info@dublin-accommodation.net
Web:	www.lucindaosullivan.com/shearwater

P ☐ NET ▱

Watersedge Hotel

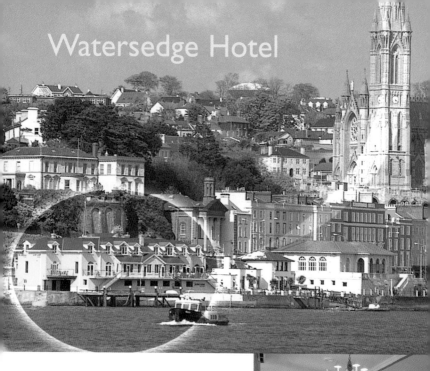

Magnificently located right in the heart of historic Cobh is the Watersedge Hotel, which title does not exaggerate in any way, for you can almost dip your toes in the Harbour waters.

The Watersedge could not be more conveniently located as it is between the old White Star Line Building and the former railway station, now the very fascinating Cobh Heritage Centre, which covers not just the history of the *Titanic*, because that of course is only part of the Cobh story, but the famine, emigration, and all the big Shipping Lines, through film shows, photos and reconstructions. One such reconstruction which really took my fancy, was that evoking a 1950's cabin showing a female passenger's luggage, the vanity case, her clothes, hairbrush, old soaps even down to a fur tie.

The hotel is bright and spacious with bedrooms with superb facilities, some even have French Doors opening out to verandahs right over the water. If you really want to treat yourself there is the suite, separate livingroom, Jacuzzi, and balcony overlooking the harbour, which has to be one of the most fab locations in the country. Yards away from our window were tugboats and a fire tender bobbing up and down reassuringly all night.Strange as it may seem it was a wonderful

experience making one feel part of the whole nautical atmosphere. We slept like logs.

When you have finished exploring Cobh you are bound to enjoy Jacob's Ladder, the hotel's brasserie style restaurant, also of course with wonderful sea views, where superb fish is the star. It is a popular place so book your table early. Breakfast too is excellent and freshly cooked. I would be very happy making the Watersedge a base while visiting Cork for you can nip across the harbour on the little Ferry from Cobh to Passage West and be in Cork City in twenty minutes or, turn left towards Carrigaline and out the back roads, to West Cork in no time at all.

So if you want to play Leonardo di Caprio to your Kate Winslet, this is definitely the place to do it!

Address:	Watersedge Hotel.
	Cobh, Co. Cork.
Tel/Fax	021 4815566/0214812011
No. Of Rooms	19
Price	
Suite	€160 - €240
DoubleTwin	€110 - €160
Single	€ 75 - €100
Family	€140 - €170
Dinner	Yes - Restaurant
Open	10th January – 23rd December
	28th December – 1st January
Credit Cards	Visa MC Amex Diners Laser
Directions.	Cobh is situated east of Cork City on the R624, off the N25 main
	Waterford to Cork Road. Follow signs for Cobh Heritage Centre.
Email:	info@watersedgehotel.ie
Web:	www.lucindaosullivan.com/watersedge

NET P

County Donegal

From the Inishowen peninsula in the north, to the sweeping beaches of the south, Donegal with its two hundred mile coastline has scenery that is unsurpassed throughout the country and is well worth a tour. Enter Donegal from the south through the popular bucket and spade holiday resort of Bundoran and travel north through Laghey before reaching Donegal Town where you may visit O'Donnell Castle. Continue around to Dunkineely with its fabulous St. John's Point and then on to Killybegs, Ireland's most successful fishing village. Onwards and upwards will bring you to Glencolumbcille and its numerous megalithic remains and nearby folk village and museum. Rejoin the N56 which winds its way northwards through Ardara, Glenties, Dungloe, and the Irish speaking Gweedore and Gortahork. The road turns southwards at Dunfanaghy, leave the N56 and go further east to the sweeping Lough Swilly and southwards through Rathmullan, to the pretty Ramelton on the banks of the salmon rich River Leannan. Continue on to Letterkenny, the county's largest town, and site of St. Eunan's Cathedral and onwards to Lifford the county town close to the Northern Ireland border town of Strabane. I should mention that Donegal has the highest seacliffs in Europe at Slieve League. Don't forget the Rosses, an area which includes Kincaslough from whence Ireland's most popular balladeer comes, and where hundreds of people flock every year to his home for the annual tea party with Daniel O'Donnell and his mother.

"A folk singer is someone who sings through his nose by ear"
(ANON)

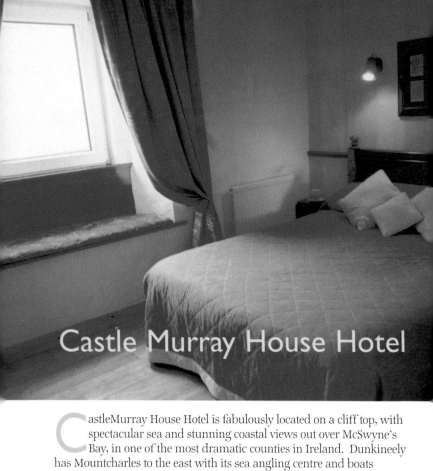

Castle Murray House Hotel

astleMurray House Hotel is fabulously located on a cliff top, with spectacular sea and stunning coastal views out over McSwyne's Bay, in one of the most dramatic counties in Ireland. Dunkineely has Mountcharles to the east with its sea angling centre and boats available for hire and, to the west, Killybegs, probably Ireland's busiest fishing village. The ruins of McSwyne's Castle are owned by the Hotel and are floodlit at night which adds to an already wonderful inherently brilliant atmosphere. The word Hotel conjures up Modern 4 Star with Leisure Centre but CastleMurray is far more intimate than that – more inns and havens feel - which are not words used very much in Ireland but do describe very well a good Restaurant with excellent accommodation and atmosphere. The ten bedrooms are all en-suite, furnished individually, and have digital T.V. and all facilities. One room is done in African style with black African carved face masks, giraffe cushions with leopard skin lampshades – you can fantasise you are on Safari though I would prefer to be here in Donegal. Another room has a pretty window seat and is beautifully decorated in colorful coral. CastleMurray is a very comfortable and relaxing spot. Have a jar in

the little bar before and after dinner – you can relax as you are not going to have to drive anywhere. Meals can be served outside on the verandah in the Summer. The food is wonderful – pick your own lobster out of a tank – prawns, scallops, crab and don't forget to finish up with the Prune and Armagnac parfait ... it is to die for.

Owners:	Marguerite Howley
Address:	St. John's Point, Dunkineely, Co. Donegal.
Tel/Fax	074 9737022/074 9737330
No. Of Rooms	10
Price	
Double/Twin	€130
Single	€90
Family	€180
Dinner	Yes - Restaurant
Open	Mid February – Mid January. Closed Monday low season. Open every day high season.
Credit Cards	Visa MC Diners Amex
Directions	2 kms from Dunkineely Village
Email:	info@castlemurray.com
Web:	www.lucindaosullivan.com/castlemurray

Coxtown Manor

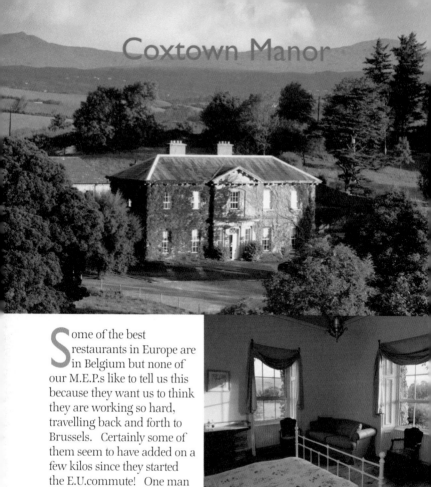

Some of the best restaurants in Europe are in Belgium but none of our M.E.P.s like to tell us this because they want us to think they are working so hard, travelling back and forth to Brussels. Certainly some of them seem to have added on a few kilos since they started the E.U.commute! One man who has come the other way and set up business in the north West, just outside Donegal Town and close to Donegal Bay, is Eduard Dewael with his fabulous late Georgian House, Coxtown Manor. The location is magnificent, the house is magnificent, the food is magnificent and service and attention are magnificent. I have not met anyone yet who has but raved about Coxtown Manor and this is a place we are going to be hearing a lot more of. The décor is very much of today, stripped floorboards, pretty colours and lovely furniture, adding a continental twist to his striking house. They have a wood panelled bar where you can try out some of the famous Belgian Strong Beers, Duval, Westmalle along with all the customary drinks. Dinner in the Restaurant offers a combination of Belgian/ Irish food or, I suppose you might say, the best of Irish produce cooked with a Belgian slant by Head Chef, Michel Aerts. Their fillet steaks are from the finest locally raised Charolais herds, the lamb is raised on Coxtown grounds, and with the

Atlantic Ocean on their doorstep, believe me the fish is good. Eduard uses free-range eggs, organic red label chicken – nothing but the best of produce. You will die for the famous Belgian chocolate desserts which feature largely on their repertoire. If you are a golfer, you have Donegal, Bundoran and Rosses Point Golf Courses from which to choose. Do a Hercule Poirot and come and investigate their Gourmet Weekends.........you won't be disappointed. Oh just think, hot chocolate with a splash of Grand Marnier before you toddle up to bed.... oh maybe I'll have another one!

Owners:	Eduard Dewael
Address:	Laghey, Co. Donegal.
Tel/Fax	07497 34575/ 07497 34576
No. Of Rooms	10
Price	
Double/Twin	€110 - €220
Single	€95 - €115
Family	Enquire
Dinner	Yes
Open	All Year except 3 weeks November and 3 weeks January.
Credit Cards	Visa MC
Directions.	Watch for sign on N15 between Ballycastle and Donegal Town.
Email:	coxtownmanor@oddpost.com
Web:	www.lucindaosullivan.com/coxtownmanor

Harvey's Point Country Hotel

In 1983 whilst on holidays from Switzerland, Jody Gysling, attracted by the stunning Swiss like snow capped Blue Stack Mountains, bought an old cottage on a swamp on the shores of Lough Eske, from two brothers by the name of Harvey. Jody gradually renovated the cottage, painstakingly drawing stones by tractor ten miles in the process. Six years later, escaping the pressures of Swiss business life, Jody and his brother Marc opened a small Guest House. A young local girl, Deirdre, took a summer job with them, romance blossomed between Deirdre and Marc and the rest, as they say, is history.

2004 was the turning point with major development and investment in Harvey's Point and what was once a tiny cottage is now a fabulous destination Hotel, nestling on the shores of shimmering Lough Eske. 42 fab new bedrooms and suites have been added in keeping with the beauty and integrity of the area. From traditional Swiss designs, the bright airy rooms feature classically comfortable wooden furniture complimented with every conceivable modern convenience. There are four categories of accommodation from which to choose, each absolutely fantastic with amazing facilities. Executive rooms have a separate foyer, kingsize beds, mini bars, Broadband Internet access. De Luxe rooms are a larger version of the Executive category. Premium suites offer all of the above along with a private dressing room,

whirlpool baths and lake views and then you have the fab Penthouse Suites double the size of the Executive Suites with bedroom, living room, bar area, lounge, dressing room, guest wc, whirlpool bath and king size bed.

Food too is a major feature at Harvey's Point. The restaurant sweeps down to the water and there is a French slant to the delicious cuisine - Donegal Bay oysters or maybe a terrine of duck foie gras flavoured with Irish Mist liqueur. Quail is boned and stuffed with morel mousse whilst shellfish and prawn bisque comes with a puff pastry lid and is embellished with a wee drop of brandy at the table. Follow up then maybe with black sole or duo of Donegal lamb, scallops or monkfish but leave room for the luscious puds.

The scenery is spectacular in Donegal and the friendliness of the people well known. Whether you land on the helicopter pad or arrive by car – get yourself to Harvey's Point – it is different and it is beautiful.

Owners:	Deirdre McGlone & Marc Gysling
Address:	Lough Eske, Donegal Town, Co. Donegal.
Tel/Fax	074 9722208/ 074 9722352
No. Of Rooms	62
Price	
Double/Twin	€178 - €290
Single	€139 - €195
Dinner	Yes
Open	All Year (Nov – March closed Sun/Mon/Tues nights)
Credit Cards	All Major Cards
Directions.	6km from Donegal Town. Follow signs for Lough Eske.
Email:	info@harveyspoint.com
Web:	

www.lucindaosullivan.com/harveyspoint

The Sandhouse Hotel
& Marine Spa

Just off the main road, between Bundoran and Donegal Town, is the magnificent sweeping beach at Rosnowlagh, on the Atlantic Coast of Donegal, where stands the lovely Sandhouse Hotel and Marine Spa. Virtually on the beach, you simply could not get any closer to sun, sea and sand!

Originally a Fishing Lodge it was transformed by the Britton family into the fine hotel it is today. Most of its bedrooms, furnished in lavish country house style, have spectacular views over Donegal Bay and its proximity to the Ocean, and its food, have always been star points. Seafood is a speciality at the aptly named Seashell Restaurant and oysters, crab, scallops, lobster, sourced from local unpolluted waters, are regularly on the menu, as well as delicious Donegal lamb, prime beef and veal, and game in season. During the day locally smoked salmon, fresh Donegal Bay oysters and mussels are also served in the cosy bar

I think we've come to realise how important it is to be able to switch off, walk the beach, and take the sea air. The Victorians used to take the waters and visit Spa towns, as did the Germans and Austrians, and way back the Romans. We are only now realising, but realising in a big way, how important water therapy is. At the Spa Suite at the Sandhouse they

offer the very best in Marine Body and Skin Care with Thalgo Marine, which uses 100% pure seaweed from the coast of Northern France. The richness of the sea oligo elements, proteins, amino acids and vitamins are captured within the Thalgo philosophy and are vital to health and well being, and ensure soft supple revitalised skin. Try the Balneotherapy, a high-powered bath with 200 water jets massaging all those tender spots like lower back and neck. Think of it, aromatic oils, mineral salts, dried seaweed. Sure, after all that toning and rejuvenation you will be running up and down the beach every day, and knocking back the champagne in the bar each evening.

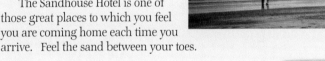

Apart from walking, surfing or just relaxing the Sandhouse is within easy reach of many championship standard golf courses and Rosnowlagh is an ideal centre from which to explore places of historical and cultural interest.

The Sandhouse Hotel is one of those great places to which you feel you are coming home each time you arrive. Feel the sand between your toes.

Owners:	The Britton Family
	Paul Diver - Manager
Address:	Rossnowlagh Beach, Rossnowlagh, Donegal Bay, Co. Donegal.
Tel/Fax	071 9851777/071 9852100
No. Of Rooms	55
Price	
Double/Twin	From €180
Single	€90
Family	€90 per adult with reductions for children
Dinner	Yes
Open	February - December
Credit Cards	All Major Cards
Directions.	From Ballyshannon take the Coast Road to Rossnowlagh.
Email:	info@sandhouse.ie
Web:	www.lucindaosullivan.com/sandhouse

NET | H | P

County Down

The County remembered in the popular Percy French Song "Where the mountains of Mourne sweep down to the sea". Apart from the Mournes, there are numerous places of interest to visit in Co. Down. North of the County is the Ulster Folk and Transport Museum one of the best in Northern Ireland. The well-known Bangor seaside resort is a popular vacation area for locals and visitors alike. Follow the shores of the beautiful Strangford Lough towards Downpatrick and its association with Ireland's Patron Saint, St. Patrick. The County offers a range of outdoor activities, walking, pony trekking, fishing and golfers will be undoubtedly be lured by Newcastle's Royal County Down Golf Course. Hillsborough Castle, where the Anglo Irish Agreement, was signed in 1985 is now the residence of the British Secretary of State for Northern Ireland and tours of the castle are available between April and September. Centred round a beautiful cathedral founded in 500AD, Dromore has a Celtic Cross, town stocks and a Victorian Viaduct.

Give me my Golf Clubs, fresh air and a beautiful partner, and you can keep my golf clubs and the fresh air!

(Jack Benny).

Clanmurry

John and Sara McCorkell's Clanmurry is a lovely peaceful traditional Georgian house on six acres of stunning gardens filled with abundant lush shrubs and plants It is a superb house in which to base oneself for visiting Northern Ireland, as it is not far from the border, only four miles from Hillsborough Castle, close to Lough Neagh, and, most importantly, very convenient for the hustle and bustle of Belfast City which is only 20 miles, and 30 minutes, down the A1. Just think of the bliss of escaping city noise and returning to such a glorious haven, or stopping there on the way to the Larne Ferry. Two twin bedrooms with garden views are serenely furnished and John and Sara are delightfully humorous hosts who will be very happy to plan out routes for you. Very interestingly the McCorkell family owned a passenger shipping line whose ships took thousands of emigrants across the Atlantic to a new life in America and Canada in the 18th and 19th Centuries. Oil paintings in Clanmurry depict the ships owned by the McCorkell Line of Derry, including the beautiful Mohongo, which made over one hundred crossings of the North Atlantic without serious mishap. The Minnehaha was the McCorkell Line's finest clipper and was known at most ports from Quebec to New Orleans as "The Green Yacht from Derry". There are many Restaurants nearby, probably best booked in advance as they are very popular, and John and Sara will be happy to organize a taxi if you don't want to drive. Breakfast at Clanmurry is brilliant so forget the old Irish Breakfast when you can be spoiled with

Coddled egg or Smoked Haddock, on its own or with a poached egg, or the real Clanmurry specialty, Kedgeree (minimum 2 people) – bring someone, drag someone but have the Kedgeree you won't get it anywhere else – very Out of Africa– or was it India....   Children Over 12 welcome.

Owners:	John & Sara McCorkell
Address:	16 Lower Quilly Road, Dromore, Co. Down BT25 1NL
Tel/Fax	+44(0)2892693760/+44(0)2892698106
No. Of Rooms	2
Price	
Double/Twin	Stg£65
Single	Stg£45
Dinner	No
Open	January 2nd – December 20th
Credit Cards	Visa MC
Directions.	Off M1 take A1 south to Dromore for 8 miles. 1st Right after road bridge over Dromore bypass. Entrance first on right.
Email:	mccorkell@btinternet.com
Web:	www.lucindaosullivan.com/clanmurry

County Dublin

County Dublin is dominated by Ireland's Capital City, Dublin. The city exudes the style and confidence of any European Capital but its citizens still know how to party and enjoy themselves like there was no tomorrow. Set on the fine sweep of Dublin Bay, the city is divided by the River Liffey, which flows from west to east. South of the river are the fine examples of Dublin's Georgian past with the lovely Fitzwilliam and Merrion Squares, and the beautiful St. Stephen's Green with its rich and colourful flowerbeds, green lawns, dreamy ponds and shaded walkways. North of the river is the Municipal Art Gallery, the Writers Museum, as well as the Phoenix Park, one of the largest enclosed parks in the world and the residence of the Country's President and the U.S. Ambassador – a favourite haunt of Dubliners. The city abounds with places and buildings that remind us of Ireland's historic and troubled past. The General Post Office was the scene of violent fighting in 1916. Dublin Castle was seat of the British Occupation Control, and Kilmainham Jail has many shadows of the past. Round the Bay to the South the road leads through fashionable Monkstown with its crescent of lively restaurants, on to the town of Dun Laoire with its harbour and yacht clubs, to Sandycove and its association with James Joyce. Further South is the magnificent sweep of Killiney Beach and the homes of many rich and famous. North of the city are some lovely and friendly seaside towns and villages – the very fashionable Malahide, the busy fishing town of Howth, the fine sandy beach of Portmarnock with its famous Golf Links and Skerries, a favourite spot for Dubliners and visitors alike. As the song says ... Dublin can be Heaven.

> "Other people have a nationality, the Irish and the Jews have a psychosis"
>
> (Brendan Behan)

Aberdeen Lodge

You won't find any "Basil Fawlty's" at Pat Halpin's Aberdeen Lodge, in the heart of Dublin's leafy embassy belt, Ballsbridge. Pat, the ultimate Hotelier, quietly misses nothing, is supremely helpful and efficient whilst, seemingly effortlessly, running four small private Hotels. Nothing is too much trouble for the staff at Aberdeen who are motivated to provide the 5 star standard of friendliness and helpfulness expected by the Head Man. Aberdeen Lodge is a large Edwardian Villa on its own grounds expertly converted to provide accommodation of the very highest standard. Fine bedrooms, some with four-posters and whirpool spa baths, have Satellite T.V. Mineral Water, trouser press, all the little details. There is an elegant drawingroom with plenty to read and you can order from their substantial Drawingroom and Room Service Menu. They also have a wine list. Breakfast is brilliant – a lavish buffet displayed in pretty Nicholas Mosse pottery followed by a hot selection. Breakfast is included in the room rate but if you want to have a business meeting over breakfast you can invite a guest to join you. Ballsbridge is where the Royal Dublin Society have their magnificent Showgrounds and is the venue of the famous Dublin Horse Show. Down the road is Lansdowne Road – the headquarters of Irish rugby. If you are a resident and your address is "Dublin 4" that says it all about you – money – class - although nowadays there is a fair scattering of nouveaux Celtic Tiger money types infiltrating the red bricked roads. Location, location, location is the story at Ballsbridge, for you can walk into the centre of Town in 15 minutes, the DART

station is nearby at Sydney Parade or taxis will be reasonable as it is so close to Town. The Blue Airport Coach also stops at two Hotels in Ballsbridge so transport is a dream. Cap that all with lots of nearby Restaurants, Thai, Indian, Chinese, French, Mediterranean and you can see what I mean about location. Not suitable for Children under 5. In Dublin for Shopping, Theatre, Rugby Matches, Business or just a break – Aberdeen Lodge is where it is at.

Owners:	Pat Halpin
Address:	53 Park Avenue, Ballsbridge, Dublin. 4.
Tel/Fax	01 283 8155/01 2837877
No. Of Rooms	19
Price	
Suite	€225 - €295
Double/Twin	€130 - €160
Single	€90 - €125
Dinner	Drawingroom Menu
Open	All Year
Credit Cards	Visa MC Amex Diners
Directions.	Down the road from Sydney Parade DART Station. Park Avenue runs parallel with Merrion Road and Strand Road close to RDS.
Email:	aberdeen@iol.ie
Web:	www.lucindaosullivan.com/aberdeenlodge

Conrad Hotel Dublin

There was a time in Dublin when the Hotels in which to be seen were the old Hibernian Hotel on Dawson Street and, way back before my time, the Russell Hotel on St Stephen's Green long since gone.

Those were the days of big Hollywood stars. We had all heard of Elizabeth Taylor being married at 18 to Hotel magnate Conrad Hilton's son, Nicky, just as we hear talk today of Paris Hilton, so there was a great air of excitement and whiff of glamour in Dublin when the Conrad Dublin opened in 1989. It was the first international Hotel to have opened in the City in 30 years and was an immediate success.

Superbly located on Earlsfort Terrace, just off St. Stephen's Green, facing the National Concert Hotel, the 5 Star Conrad Dublin is just a few minutes walk from fashionable Grafton Street. It is also very convenient for the National Gallery, Trinity College, the National Museum and Georgian Dublin. I did an article not so long ago on Hotel Lobbies and the interesting people who frequented them for coffee or drinks and, in the Conrad, I nearly fell backwards trying to overhear the conversation between a well known Irish Builder and Politician. ......Unfortunately I will never know the outcome! So it is always worth keeping your eyes open in the Conrad because there are lots of famous people who've stayed there, including Billy Connolly, Mimi Rogers, Rod Stewart and Senator Hilary Clinton.

A major refurbishment programme costing €15m has just been completed and the hotel now offers 192 spacious guest rooms along with 24-hour room service, a fitness centre and an underground car park. Their new urban cool Alex Restaurant and Bar specialises in really good seafood so you can indulge yourself in caviar or lobster, but do try the brown shrimp risotto which is sublime. A glass screen links the restaurant to the Cocktail Bar and, oh boy, can I testify to the fact that the cocktails are stunners! The Hotel also has a traditional Irish Pub, "Alfie Byrne's", named after a much loved Lord Mayor, popular with Dubliners as well as hotel guests, doing excellent pub food.

The level of service at the Conrad is amazing and, coupled with everything else I have told you, it is a really Great Place to Stay in Dublin, I love that frisson of glam...

Owners:	Laurens Zieren (General Manager)
Address:	Earlsfort Terrace, Dublin. 2.
Tel/Fax	01 602 8900/01 602 5424
No. Of Rooms	192
Price	
Double/Twin	€185-€275
Single	€185-€275
Family	€45 Supplement to above rates for extra bed in room.
Dinner	Yes – Restaurant and Bar food
Open	All Year
Credit Cards	Visa MC Amex Diners Laser
Directions.	From Dublin Airport, take the MI/NI to the City Centre. Follow signs to St. Stephen's Green. Hotel Located off St. Stephen's Green opposite National Concert Hall.
Email:	dublininfo@conradhotels.com
Web:	www.lucindaosullivan.com/conradhotel

Looking for that perfect little *pied a terre* hideaway for a stay in Dublin? Well Drummond Mews is it. Located in Dublin's exclusive suburb of Monkstown, close to the sea, yacht clubs, the fashionable restaurants of Monkstown, Blackrock, Dun Laoire and Dalkey, Drummond Mews is an original coach house mews to a large Victorian house. Drummond Mews is beside Dun Laoire Golf Club and close to many others. Totally independent and secluded, Drummond Mews has its own private high-walled secure drive in courtyard where one can dine al fresco, take the sun or just sit and hear the birds sing. The bedroom is very prettily furnished and decorated with Farrow & Ball colours, bath ensuite (wash-basin, w.c. and bath).

Downstairs has a large Mediterranean style tiled living cum dining area with small but more than pleasing galley kitchen, fully equipped with microwave, washer-dryer. There is also satellite T.V. and all bed linen and towels are supplied free of charge.

Dublin Tourism 3 Star graded. 10 minutes walk to the DART station, which whisks you into central Dublin in 15 minutes and the 46A bus runs from the top of the road serving U.C.D. Drummond Mews is also very convenient for the Sandyford/Stillorgan Estate for people on temporary assignments to Dublin and has easy access to the M50.

Owners:	Mary O'Sullivan
Address:	Monkstown, Co. Dublin
Tel/Fax	01 2800419
No. Of Rooms	Mews House sleeps 2
Price	€595 - €625 per week
Dinner	Self Catering
Open	All Year
Credit Cards	Visa MC
Directions.	Phone above
Email:	info@dublin-accommodation.net
Web:	www.lucindaosullivan.com/drummondmews

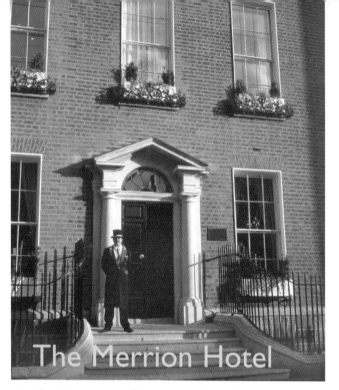

The Merrion Hotel

During the 18th century, Dublin was transformed from a mediaeval town into one of the finest Georgian cities in Europe. The 5 Star Merrion Hotel, which opened in 1997, is set in the heart of Georgian Dublin, opposite Government Buildings and comprises four meticulously restored Grade 1 Georgian townhouses and a specially commissioned garden wing around private period gardens. Built in 1760 the most important of these houses is Mornington House, birthplace of the 1st Duke of Wellington. Quite magnificently structured, the doors, architraves, the intricate delicate fanlights, heavy staircases, and amazing rococo plasterwork are just a pleasure to absorb.

Dubliners have clasped The Merrion to their bosom for a splendidly gracious atmosphere has been maintained whilst being elegantly unstuffy. The interior is designed using Irish fabrics and antiques reflecting the original interiors. The public rooms are welcoming and serene – particularly the Drawingrooms and terrace - where one can sit and have afternoon tea or a drink in the most civilized of surroundings, whilst also enjoying one of the finest private collections of 19th and 20th century Art for works by Mary Swanzy, Roderic O'Conor, Sir John

Lavery, Paul Henry, and many more, are set against this beautiful backdrop.

There are two in-house restaurants - Patrick Guilbaud's, the superb Michelin 2 starred establishment and the beautiful Cellar Restaurant, with its cool uplit vault style columns and pale tiled floor. Here too the food is sublime and very reasonably priced apart at all from the fact that you are sitting in one of the finest 5 star hotels in Ireland.

The restoration of The Merrion demanded the highest standards and the designers' brief was both simple and clear - "To create a space with sensitivity to the 18th century heritage of the building with light and airy bedrooms". As a result, the guest rooms and suites are the epitome of elegance and also supremely inviting and comfortable, not to mention the most spectacular Penthouse Suite in Dublin.

There is also the beautiful Tethra Spa which offers a comprehensive choice of bodycare and beauty treatments using exclusive E'SPA products so this is just the place to relax after a hard day shopping in nearby Grafton Street or visiting the National Gallery and Museums just across the way.

The Merrion Hotel is Heaven on Earth – nothing more, nothing less.

Owners:	Peter McCann
	– General Manager
Address:	Upper Merrion Street, Dublin 2.
Tel/Fax	01 6030600/01 6030700
No. Of Rooms	143
Price	
Double/Twin	From €390
Dinner	Yes – 2 Restaurants
Open	All Year
Credit Cards	All Major Credit Cards
Directions.	From the top of Grafton Street, turn left, continue on straight and take the third turn left on to Upper Merrion Street.
Email:	info@merrionhotel.com
Web:	www.lucindaosullivan.com/merrionhotel

Radisson SAS St. Helen's Hotel

The 5 Star Radisson SAS St. Helen's Hotel is the only hotel in Ireland's capital city to be set within 4 acres of magnificent formal gardens and as, happily, I live not too far from the Hotel, it happens to be one of my favourite spots. There is nothing else like it in Dublin, let alone in the surrounding suburban areas - an oasis of good food, hospitality and value.

St. Helen's, one of Ireland's finest historic houses, has been meticulously and sympathetically restored to provide superb accommodation and it is equally convenient to the centre of Dublin, the Wicklow mountains, the M50 and Sandyford Industrial Estate and the nearby Yacht Clubs of Dun Laoghaire, and you have no worries about parking your car in their big free car park, always an important factor when visiting a strange City.

The guest rooms are superb, large and spacious and, most unusually, Radisson Hotels allow 2 children up to 17 years to share their parent's room free of charge, for each bedroom has two queen-sized beds.   Now, that is a major attraction for families with children who once they reach 12 years of age generally have to pay adult rates. They may be 6ft 2" giants at that stage but they are still expensive children if you have to pay full whack!

Apart from all of those advantages, probably the best Italian Restaurant in Dublin is situated in the Radisson St. Helen's in the form of its Talavera Restaurant.   It has the most amazing antipasti table with an enormous selection of Italian charcuterie, marinated vegetables and all sorts of delicious goodies to be enjoyed as a starter or main course. They

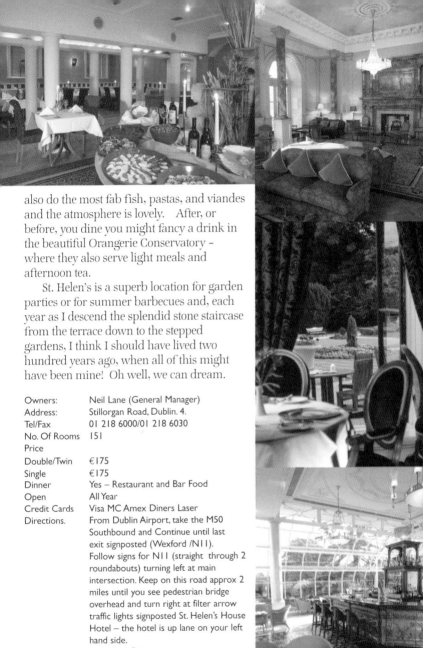

also do the most fab fish, pastas, and viandes and the atmosphere is lovely. After, or before, you dine you might fancy a drink in the beautiful Orangerie Conservatory – where they also serve light meals and afternoon tea.

St. Helen's is a superb location for garden parties or for summer barbecues and, each year as I descend the splendid stone staircase from the terrace down to the stepped gardens, I think I should have lived two hundred years ago, when all of this might have been mine! Oh well, we can dream.

Owners:	Neil Lane (General Manager)
Address:	Stillorgan Road, Dublin. 4.
Tel/Fax	01 218 6000/01 218 6030
No. Of Rooms	151
Price	
Double/Twin	€175
Single	€175
Dinner	Yes – Restaurant and Bar Food
Open	All Year
Credit Cards	Visa MC Amex Diners Laser
Directions.	From Dublin Airport, take the M50 Southbound and Continue until last exit signposted (Wexford /N11). Follow signs for N11 (straight through 2 roundabouts) turning left at main intersection. Keep on this road approx 2 miles until you see pedestrian bridge overhead and turn right at filter arrow traffic lights signposted St. Helen's House Hotel – the hotel is up lane on your left hand side.
Email:	info.dublin@radissonsas.com
Web:	

www.lucindaosullivan.com/radissonsthelens

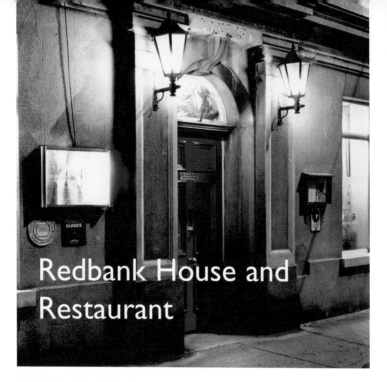

Redbank House and Restaurant

SKERRIES, CO. DUBLIN.

Skerries is a fishing village north of Dublin which is forever in my heart as I spent summers there as a child. It all now seems so simple and real. We would swim on the sandy shore of the south beach be it rain or shine. I still remember being enveloped in a big soft towel and dried off on a wet day whilst the aroma of the frying chips and salt were blown down the beach. My mother would buy prawns from the fishermen while my father slipped into the Stoop Your Head or Joe May's for a pint and a half one, which is the colloquialism for a Pint of Guinness and a whiskey. Daddy would then have a smile on his chops as Mother and I would drop the live prawns into the boiling pot for a whisker of a second, take them out and eat them with salt. The local Cinema heralded the delights of Lilac Time with Anna Neagle warbling "we'll gather lilacs in the spring again" ... it was a hundred years old then and it seems like a thousand years old now ... but Skerries at its heart still retains a wonderful untouched sense of the real Ireland for it is largely undiscovered by tourists.

REDBANK HOUSE AND RESTAURANT

The Redbank House and Restaurant is owned and run by one of Ireland's best-known Chefs, Terry McCoy. Terry is a familiar figure on the Irish foodie scene, not just because he is a striking figure who sports

a ponytail and beard but because he wins awards all round him for his handling of very fine seafood caught off the Fingal coast. Whilst the Redbank Restaurant has been a destination Restaurant for the past 20 years or so it is only in the past couple of years that Terry added 18 rooms. The rooms are comfortably furnished with all mod cons and comforts in cool nautical colours, blues, yellows and cream, but with a warmth of feeling. All have T.V. and Internet access. This is a house too for the Gourmet Golfer, for there are forty golf courses within "a driver and a sand wedge" of Skerries and what is better after a quick one at the 19th hole than to come back to enjoy Terry's hospitality and fabulous treatment of our wonderful Dublin Bay Prawns and other seafood. Try the Razor fish, caught locally, which are mainly exported to Japan and also ask the see the wine cellar in the old Bank Vault. The Redbank's long Sunday lunches are legendary. St. Patrick who drove the snakes out of Ireland lived on Church Island off Skerries and fed himself on goat's milk and goats cheese so you see chevre was popular in Skerries before anywhere else in Ireland! Skerries is only 18 miles from Dublin, easily commutable by train, and is only 20 minutes drive from Dublin Airport so a perfect way to start or finish your holiday in Ireland Walk the beaches; feel the sea breeze in your hair and the sand between your toes, chill out, it is the place.

 NET P

Owners:	Terry McCoy
Address:	5-7 Church Street, Skerries, Co. Dublin.
Tel/Fax	01 849 1005/01 849 1598
No. Of Rooms	18
Price	
Double/Twin	€120
Single	€75
Family	€120 + €25 per extra person including breakfast
Dinner	Yes - Restaurant
Open	All Year – Restaurant closed for dinner Sunday nights, and also 24th, 25th and 26th December.
Credit Cards	All major cards
Directions.	Opposite AIB Skerries
Email:	info@redbank.ie
Web:	www.lucindaosullivan.com/redbankhouse

County Galway

As a county, Galway encompasses a University City, the wild splendour and magnificence of Connemara and the Twelve Bens then, to cap it all, you have the Aran Islands. Galway City has a vibrancy all of its own and straddles the Corrib river which thunders down under the Salmon Weir Bridge and winds itself around the City to the lively pedestrianised Quay Street at Wolfe Tone Bridge, where the river enters the famous Galway Bay.   Worth seeing is the Spanish Arch, a 16th century structure used to protect galleons unloading wine and rum – most important - and the Collegiate Church of St. Nicholas of Myra, the largest mediaeval church in Ireland, built in 1320 dedicated to the patron saint of sailors. It is almost impossible to find a bed in Galway during Race Week, the Arts Festival, and the Oyster Festival at Clarinbridge so book early. The City abounds with Art Galleries and here you can also visit the home of Nora Barnacle, wife of James Joyce, which is now a small museum. Beyond the Claddagh village from which originated the Claddagh ring – is Salthill - the more honky tonk holiday area with amusement arcades. Moving west around the coast

"A good holiday is one spent among people whose
notions of time are vaguer than yours"
(J.B. Priestly)

road you come to An Spideal or Spiddle, the heart of the Gaeltacht. Inland is Oughterard, a long pretty village on the River Owenriff, which is very popular with anglers. Oughterard is the gateway to Connemara but a wonderful base for a holiday or break for those who want to have easy access to Galway City. Clifden is the capital of Connemara and is laid out in a triangle. Small and compact but with wide streets and buildings perched high above the deep estuary of the River Owenglin, Clifden is renowned for its Connemara Pony Show. Many famous Irish artists, Paul Henry, Maurice MacGonigal, Jack Yeats, and Sean Keating, have immortalized Clifden in their paintings. The Alcock & Brown Memorial, which commemorates the first transatlantic flight in 1919, is worth seeing. Ten miles northeast of Clifden is Letterfrack, a 19th century Quaker village and just northwest of that is the magnificent Renvyle peninsula, which has strong literary associations.

Delphi Mountain Resort And Spa

S et amidst the wild and rugged beauty of the Delphi Valley, on 300 acres of forested estate, Delphi Mountain Resort and Spa is a haven of tranquillity and peace not to be missed. It could only happen in Ireland for Delphi is actually in South Mayo but its postal address is County Galway! Fresh clean unpolluted air, magical scenery, and crystal clear water await the visitor. The Lodge, designed to fit into the surrounding landscape, is built in local stone and wood with large bay windows enveloping the scenic beauty with many bedrooms having patios. Loft Suites are individually themed and decorated in timbers of oak, ash and elm. The dining room serves delicious meals, with organically grown garden vegetables and locally caught fresh fish. There is also a good wine list and a comfortable cocktail bar. We are only now realising how much Spas can do for our well being and Delphi is superb. Imagine having treatments in a darkened womblike beehive shaped room. Scented candles gently glow and soft relaxing music plays, while a therapist devotes herself to your needs with treatments for the face, body and feet, with a range of massage - Aromatherapy, Swedish, Sports, Reflexology,

Indian Head Massage.... Body wraps using seaweed extracts and marine clay are very popular. Body exfoliation rids the dead skin cells, balneotherapy treatments detox, and anti-cellulite treatments help rid the body of toxins and orange-peel skin. Enjoy the spectacular views of the Mweelrea mountain range, with its dramatic snow capped tips, from the large bubbling Jacuzzi whilst overhead stars twinkle. No wonder Delphi has been voted one of the top 10 spas in the world by Conde Nast and was the winner of the Irish Beauty Industry awards. For those who

want an active holiday as well as a relaxing time, there is The Great Outdoors Option, where walking, either power or hill walking, biking, kayaking, canoeing, hiking strength training, Tai Chi or yoga, surfing, pony trekking, abseiling, sailing, high ropes course, are all available during your stay. We cycled into Leenane, passing the areas where The Quiet Man was filmed and took a boat trip along Kilary Harbour, the only fjord in Ireland. Otters, Cormorants, wild duck and herons are seen in abundance and there are also fab dolphin watching trips. Magical.

Owners:	Pat Shaughnessy
Address:	Leenane, Co. Galway.
Tel/Fax	095 42208/095 42303
No. Of Rooms	22
Price	
Double/Twin	€290
Single	€180
Dinner	Yes
Open	January 8th to December 8th
Credit Cards	All Major Cards
Directions.	Take N59 to Leenane then it is 7 miles to Delphi
Email:	delphigy@iol.ie
Web:	www.lucindaosullivan.com/delphimountainresort

Galway Radisson SAS Hotel and Spa

The Galway Radisson SAS Hotel and Spa is to the Hotel Industry what the Lamborghini is to the Motor biz! Sleek in design, powerful in body, the Galway Radisson just purrs. Established in 2001, this 4 Star hotel is only five minutes walk from Eyre Square but boasts fabulous views of Lough Atalia and Galway Bay. The magnificent glass Atrium of the hotel's foyer sets the scene of lightness and clarity within. The stylish Atrium Bar and Lounge with tinkling piano opens out onto a heated terrace where you can have a drink and watch "the sun go down on Galway Bay". The rooms are pretty fab – 217 in total in various categories and with three room styles: Maritime, Scandinavian, or Classic. There are Standard, Superior, Business Class, Junior Suites, Executive Suites and Rooms catering for people with a disability. All rooms have a Power Tower, a space saving device that offers satellite television with movie channels, coffee/tea-maker, minibar, personal safe ... whilst the Executive Suites represent the world's highest technological standards. If you really want to splash out Level 5 is top drawer - where Guests are guaranteed privacy and personal service in 16 spacious luxurious executive rooms. Included in Level 5 is a Club Lounge, complimentary treats served throughout the day, soft drinks and canapés during Club Hour, secure membership only access, panoramic rooftop terrace, free use of the Business Service Centre and a separate meeting room... The stylish split level 220 seater Restaurant Marina is a vision of blue, integrated with dark walnut, reflecting the nautical theme and, as Galway is famous for its seafood, that is the specialty – Galway Bay Oysters, Scallops, Lobster, Monkfish – but there are delicious carnivorous options too. Chill out in the Spirit

One Spa with facilities found only in the best destination Spas in the world - Sabia Med, Hammam, Rocksauna, Aroma Grotto, Tropical Rain Shower, Cold Fog Showers, Ice Drench and Heated Loungers. The Leisure Centre's Swimming Pool is fab along with children's Pool, Jacuzzi, Sauna, Outdoor Canadian Hot Tub. How could you beat that – Radisson Galway is fantastic.

Owners:	Tom Flanagan (General Manager)
Address:	Lough Atalia Road, Galway.
Tel/Fax	091 538300/091 538380
No. Of Rooms	217
Price	
Double/Twin	€240
Single	€220
Family	€269
Dinner	Yes
Open	All Year
Credit Cards	All Major Cards
Directions.	5 minutes from Eyre Square on Lough Atalia waterfront.
Email:	reservations.galway@radissonsas.com
Web:	www.lucindaosullivan.com/radissongalway

Great Southern Hotel Galway

W hen I think of all the youngsters taking off now to far flung places immediately after their Leaving Certificate exams, it brings me back to my first trip away from home with a pal. It was all very daring – we went to Salthill for three days! She was a very prissy sort of girl who insisted on wearing white gloves walking along the prom! We, of course, were staying in a very simple B & B and had to walk in and out to the centre of the City but, the first place we headed for was the imposing Great Southern Hotel on Eyre Square. Boy, was I impressed ... the magnificent high ceilings and plasterwork, the fabulous reception areas ... We were totally intimidated at that age by the grandeur of it all but I have never forgotten it.

I have great time for Great Southern Hotels and I have had great times in Great Southern Hotels. They offer a splendour and graciousness that modern Hotels just cannot buy and the Galway GSH's unparalleled location and splendour has meant that it has been an

integral part of the social life of Galway City since 1845 – when guests would in fact have worn white gloves!!

In the past couple of years, GSH Galway has undergone a restoration programme which has combined the magnificent old world features of the hotel with new age facilities, delivering a new level of luxury and opulence. There is a splendid new marble floored lobby, open fire, glistening chandeliers and a range of bedrooms – standard, executive, junior and senior suites. All have modem/pc connections, interactive TV systems whilst suites also have a spacious dressing room, work area, mini bar and CD music system.

There is also a new Spa and Health Club on the fifth floor called The Square so, having walked the feet off yourself around the City of the Tribes, you can come back and treat yourself to a Hot Stone Massage or chill out in the Outdoor Canadian Hot Tub. There is always a buzz and action in their Cocktail Bar, Croi Na G, and here you will meet the movers and shakers of the City whilst downstairs is the casual and fun O'Flaherty's Basement Bar. Have a drink in either before you head into the Oyster Room Restaurant – the food is superb and you will always feel you are somewhere special.

General Manager:	Richard Collins
Address:	Eyre Square, Galway.
Tel/Fax	091 564041/091 566704
No. Of Rooms	99
Price	
Double/Twin	From €160
Single	From €160
Dinner	Yes - Restaurant
Open	All Year
Credit Cards	Visa MC Amex Diners Laser
Directions.	City Centre on Eyre Square
Email:	res@galway-gsh.com
Web:	www.lucindaosullivan.com/gshgalway

Renvyle House Hotel

"**M**y house...stands on a lake, but it stands also on the sea – waterlillies meet the golden seaweed. It is as if, in the faery land of Connemara at the extreme end of Europe, the incongruous flowed together at last, and the sweet and bitter blended. Behind me, islands and mountainous mainland share in a final reconciliation, at this, the world's end". So wrote Oliver St. John Gogarty in 1927 of his then home. Spectacularly located nestling between the blue Twelve Bens mountain range and the Shores of the Atlantic Ocean, Renvyle has a tremendous history and it has always attracted famous people from all over the world. The house has been pulled down, rebuilt, burnt to ashes, rebuilt again. It has been home to Donal O'Flaherty, Chieftan of one of the oldest and most powerful Clans of Connaught, and to Mrs. Caroline Blake who was the first to open it as a hotel way back in 1883. But, enough of the past, for Renvyle has been a hotel for all seasons and has always moved with the times and now in 2006 is a stylish destination which is hugely popular with the Irish public, who return again and again for blissful respite and evenings filled with fun. Situated on a 200 acre Estate, Renvyle has a lake teaming with trout, a heated outdoor pool, a 9-hole golf course and its own beach. There is clay pigeon shooting, horse riding in season, and buckets of activities and creche facilities during holiday periods. Pets are allowed "within reason" – enquire - for that doesn't mean Pooch can sit up with his Cartier collar at the dining table! Throughout the year there are Painting Breaks, Murder Mystery Weekends, Fly Fishing instruction, Golf Breaks and Walking Breaks. Sixty- eight bedrooms and five suites, are spacious and very comfortable

with all that even the most difficult guest could possibly desire. Excellent food is based on fresh local produce, Connemara lamb, game, fresh fish. In fact Renvyle Chef, Tim O'Sullivan, is a winner of the Moreau Chablis fish cookery competition. Classical Pianist, Derek Hoffman, accompanies dinner each evening, on Count John McCormack's Steinway Grand Piano – playing it that is! Oh, I want to get in the car and drive there again this minute ... Ronnie Counihan runs a great house...

Owner:	John Coyle
Chief Executive	Ronnie Counihan
Address:	Renvyle, Connemara, Co. Galway.
Tel/Fax	095 43511/095 43515
No. Of Rooms	68
Price	
Double/Twin	From €120
Single	From €60
Family	From €140 (2 Adults + 2 Children)
Dinner	Yes
Open	February – January
Credit Cards	All Major Cards
Directions.	Take N59 from Galway to Renvyle. Hotel signposted in village.
Email:	info@renvyle.com
Web:	www.lucindaosullivan.com

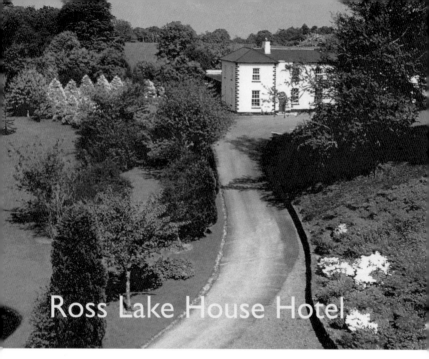

Ross Lake House Hotel

Fancy waking up in a four-poster bed in a splendid Georgian house, on 6 acres of rambling woods and rolling lawns, in the magnificent wilderness of Connemara, then Henry and Elaine Reid's Ross Lake House Hotel is for you. Ross Lake House was formerly part of the Killaguile estate built by James Edward Jackson, land agent for Lord Iveagh at Ashford Castle, but renamed as a Country House Hotel because of its proximity to Ross Lake and the fishing waters of Lough Corrib. With 13 spacious guestrooms and suites, all beautifully and individually designed to reflect the charm and graciousness of the house, yet provide the modern facilities we all expect nowadays, you will be very comfortable.

There are lovely classic rooms oozing with country house charm, fabulous superior rooms with period furniture and luxurious fabrics, and then, stunning suites with their own sitting area. As pretty Oughterard is only 22 km from Galway City it is ideal for visiting the vibrancy that is Galway,

but choosing to leave it when you wish. There are Golf Courses all round – Oughterard, Barna, Galway Bay and Ballyconneely Links Course so if he wants to swing a club you can take off to the Antique shops. You are also ideally poised at Ross Lake for doing the rugged wilder aspects of the Connemara of "The Quiet Man". There is a cosy library bar to snuggle into and an elegant drawingroom with blazing fires to retire to after dinner and make new friends over a nightcap of the liquid variety. The dining room is gracious and the Chef concentrates on the finest fresh produce from the Connemara hills, rivers, lakes and the Atlantic Ocean so you can expect beautiful crabmeat, wild salmon, tender lamb, scrumptious desserts and fine wines. Henry and Elaine are charming and helpful hosts and, believe me, you will really enjoy a spell at their lovely Ross Lake House.

Owners:	Henry and Elaine Reid
Address:	Rosscahill, Oughterard, Co. Galway.
Tel/Fax	091 550109/091 550184
No. Of Rooms	13
Price	
Double/Twin	€170
Single	€115
Family	€230
Dinner	Yes
Open	March 15 to October 31st
Credit Cards	All Major Cards
Directions	Follow N59 towards Clifden. Hotel signposted after Moycullen.
Email:	rosslake@iol.ie
Web:	www.lucindaosullivan.com/rosslakehousehote

County Kerry

Co. Kerry is known as "the Kingdom" and it is difficult to know where one starts to list the attractions of this amazing area. There is the world famous Killarney with its three lakes and impressive McGillycuddy Reeks looming behind them with their ever changing shades and colours. Almost as well known is the hair raising and breathtaking Ring of Kerry on the Iveragh peninsula with its sheer drops and stark coastal scenery. Coaches are required to travel anti-clockwise and leave Killarney between 10 and 11 a.m. so if you are doing it in a day, you need to be earlier or you will be behind them all day. Some books tell you to drive clockwise but it can be nerve racking if you meet a coach on a narrow pass as I have experienced. Head out to Killorglin famous for its mid-August Puck Fair where eating, drinking, dancing, singing is reigned over by the King of the Festival, a Puck Goat. From Killorglin move on taking in the beautiful Caragh Lake to Glenbeigh with Rossbeigh's sweeping beach. On to Cahersiveen and swing out via the new bridge to Valentia island. Come back and head

"A folk song is a song nobody ever wrote" (anon)

south to Waterville where Charlie Chaplin and family spent their summers. The final stage is Caherdaniel to Sneem and the lush subtropical richness of Parknasilla which is then about eighteen miles from the popular town of Kenmare. North of the county is Listowel famous for its Writers Week and generally regarded as the literary capital of Ireland but also celebrates a madly popular Horse Race Week. Tralee, the principal town of the county, is a very busy commercial centre and also hosts the famous Rose of Tralee celebration. Dingle of "Ryan's Daughter" fame is stunning and has a life of its own. It also has Fungi the dolphin. Among Kerry's many famous Championship Golf Courses is Ballybunion, the favourite haunt of American golfer, Tom Watson, who was once captain of the famous Club. Kerry has an abundance of eateries at all prices and in keeping with Irish tradition is well catered for in drinking establishments, many of which provide ballads and folk songs.

Aghadoe Heights Hotel & Spa

Aghadoe Heights Hotel at Killarney is not just any ordinary Hotel, it is a unique experience. 5 star unpretentious luxury at your fingertips, just the right distance outside the centre of the Town, directly overlooking the Killarney Lakes. The Aghadoe Heights is bliss and switch off time, from which you will only be disturbed by the solicitous and gentle pampering of the ever-attentive staff. The public rooms are furnished with a mélange of elegant eclectic pieces from the Far East, mixed through with French antiques, a fine modern Irish art collection, and sculptures. Luxurious elegant bedrooms have balconies, whilst spacious junior suites with floor to ceiling windows have fantastic quadraphonic high tech TV's as well. A Roman style indoor swimming pool is placed to the front of the building so, as you swim, you can still see the lakes and mountains with their ever changing palette of moody colours. Right next door to the pool is a new hip cocktail bar for that cool drink or you can slip upstairs to the open plan lounge and have the most scrumptious afternoon tea, served by white gloved girls.

Luxuriate in the fantastic new Aveda Spa. Try the Precious Stone Therapy – Aghadoe have the only Precious Stone Room in the world where you sit on a throne facing an amethyst grotto,

it is blissful. In the evening you will be relaxed and ready for delicious food in Frederick's Restaurant, which is incorporated in the large first floor open plan area, where the resident pianist plays away on the grand piano. They have their own lobster tank or you might fancy the best sole on the bone, or Oysters Rockefeller, or smoked fillet of venison with fresh linguine, juniper and orange jus.... To cap it all Aghadoe now has the most fantastic two bedroomed penthouse suite, with outdoor hot tub, exquisitely furnished to include pieces by style icon Eileen Gray, as well

as paintings by Maria Simmonds Gooding, and Pat Scott, and it has its own Paul Burrell – a butler who won't tell all! Chauffeur service to and from Kerry Airport available or come by helicopter. "How can you buy Killarney" were the words of the song but how can you buy Aghadoe is the real question!

Owners:	Pat & Marie Chawke (General Managers)
Address:	Aghadoe, Lakes of Killarney, Co. Kerry.
Tel/Fax	064 31766/064 31345
No. Of Rooms	97
Price	
Penthouse	€2,500
Double/Twin	€250 - €680
Single	€200 - €600
Family	€250 - €370
Dinner	Yes - Restaurant
Open	Mid March - End December
Credit Cards	All Major Cards
Directions.	2 miles west of Killarney, signposted off N22
Email:	info@aghadoeheights.com
Web:	

www.lucindaosullivan.com/aghadoeheightshotel

The Brook Lane Hotel

Kenmare is a fantastic town to which people gravitate in search of good food and fun and they will find it in abundance. Kenmare, or to give it its Irish name "Neidin", has lots of shops, boutiques, galleries, decent places to eat, and pubs by the score, you will never be bored in Kenmare.

THE BROOK LANE HOTEL

A very welcome addition to Kenmare is the stylish new boutique Brook Lane Hotel, which adds an urban chic dimension to the accommodation sector, having superb rooms and doing excellent modern food. The Brook Lane is very conveniently located on the corner of the road leading to, or from, Sneem and the Ring of Kerry, which means that you are very close to the centre of town. All you have to do is dump your car and stroll around "doing" the boutiques, galleries and pubs, without worrying whether you will find a parking space or not - Kenmare is a busy spot.

The Hotel has been done with immense panache – cool and contemporary – and unlike anywhere else that I can think of in Kenmare. It is what today's traveller wants and deserves in the line of comfort and luxury without being overly expensive. The bedrooms are gorgeous, beds to get lost in, fluffy robes and heated bathroom floors to keep your toes warm. Whether your room is Superior, Deluxe or a Junior Suite, you can't go wrong. Colours are neutral with lots of big brown leather cosy chairs to settle into and the service is excellent and friendly.

There is plenty of good casual food served all day in their cool Casey's Bar and Bistro, which is very attractively finished using lots of

brick detail, and where you can very comfortably perch at the bar for that pint or a cocktail. Having perhaps just done the Ring of Kerry you will be hungry so for dinner you can start thinking of delicious pan-fried scallops on ginger bread, followed maybe by monkfish with a chilli and coriander cream, or roast breast of Aylesbury duck on hot and sour cabbage. In summer, Irish Nights (not every night so do enquire when booking) are organised for diners and you may well get to see a Bodhran, a traditional Irish musical instrument, being played. So at The Brook Lane you will get the very best of chic modern hospitality with a bit of tradition thrown in for good measure.

Owners:	Una Brennan
Address:	Kenmare, Co. Kerry.
Tel/Fax	064 42077/064 40869
No. Of Rooms	20
Price	
Double/Twin	€110 - €190
Family	€140 - €200
Dinner	Yes – Bar food and Restaurant
Open	All Year – Closed 23rd – 27th December
Credit Cards	Visa MC Amex Diners Laser
Directions.	On the corner at the junction of the N70/N71
Email:	info@brooklanehotel.com
Web:	www.lucindaosullivan.com/brooklanehotel

The Butler Arms Hotel

As you drive down into Waterville, on the southern point of the Ring of Kerry, there is an air of stillness, lushness and beauty. Waterville looks out to the Atlantic but there is also an unspoken eternal sultry drama and amazing colour to the backdrop of mountains. Perhaps this is what appealed to one of the most famous movie stars of all time, Charlie Chaplin, who every summer took his large family here for their annual holidays. With undoubted good taste, they stayed at the Butler Arms Hotel spectacularly located right in the middle of Waterville with views that no set designer could ever recreate.

Over the years the hotel has been upgraded with the same impeccable taste that made it famous in the first place. Their enviable register reads like a roll-call of the famous including Catherine Zeta Jones, Michael Douglas, Dan Marino, as well as former US Vice President Dan Quail and, with Waterville's Championship Golf Links being a Mecca for golfers, Tiger Woods has also stayed, not to mention that the hotel was a favourite place of the late Payne Stewart.

I love everything about the Butler Arms, the beautifully restrained and impeccable bedrooms, the Charlie Chaplin lounge where I crash out and catch up on my reading, breaking for a casual lunch in the Fisherman's Bar, but saving myself somewhat for the goodies that will be available in the Fisherman's Restaurant for Dinner! The food is excellent and you can indulge yourself with lobster or wild salmon from Lough Currane or, if you are a real carnivore, there is the best of Kerry

Mountain lamb ....the menu is always extensive and you won't be disappointed.

So don't just whiz around the Ring of Kerry like the coach tours, make Waterville your destination and stay and enjoy its spectacular beauty and interesting spots. The home of the Emancipator, Daniel O'Connell, just six miles away at Derrynane Bay is well worth a visit and there are dozens of ancient forts and standing stones. Ballinskelligs too is nearby or you could take a boat trip to the Skelligs.

Whatever you do you will have a wonderful time at the Butler Arms.

Owners:	Peter and Mary Huggard	
Address:	Waterville, Co. Kerry.	
Tel/Fax	066 9474144/066 9474520	
No. Of Rooms	40	
Price		
Junior Suite	€250/€350	
Double/Twin	€140/€200	
Dinner	Restaurant and Bar Food	
Open	April to October	
Credit Cards	Visa MC Amex Laser	
Directions.	In the centre of Waterville	
Email:	reservations@butlerarms.com	
Web:	www.lucindaosullivan.com/butlerarms	

Cahernane House Hotel

My first introduction to the Cahernane House Hotel was over twenty years ago when my better half and I went there for a weekend. At that stage some German people owned it. I particularly remember our lovely room to the back of the house with ivy-clad walls, overlooking beautiful countryside and lawns. We decided to go for a stroll around the grounds but discovered that there was a pet fox in a wire compound and apparently he was on a diet of live rabbit, which ended our stroll rather rapidly! Since that time of course things have changed in a big way. It is now a spankingly beautiful Country House Hotel stunningly located and I have always had a great affection for it.

The former home of the Earls of Pembroke this gorgeous old historic house is at the end of the long tree-lined drive sheltered away from the world yet close to everything, just like being on one's own private estate. The Earls of Pembroke came to Ireland in 1656. One brother was given the great Muckross Estate and the other the smaller property of Currens and Cahernane, and they maintained these magnificent Estates for five generations. In 1877 the original house was considered outmoded, torn down and replaced with the beautiful house which stands today.

Located on the Kenmare road just 1.5 kms from Killarney town centre, Cahernane House has undergone a magnificent but sympathetic refurbishment providing the ultimate in luxury, including suites and junior suites, and superb modern rooms in a new section. Do note the beautiful latticed staircase and scrumptious drawing room, they are really beautiful. Food is excellent too in their Herbert Room Restaurant. We had delicious pan-fried medallions of veal with a wild mushroom and garlic mustard cream on our visit followed by scrumptious pear and almond tart. The wine list is extensive and they also do excellent casual food in the Cellar Bar – delicious seafood chowder, white crabmeat salad and also a lovely Country House Salad of mixed leaves, smoked bacon, poached egg, and asparagus Being run now by the Brown family, Cahernane House Hotel has the benefit of personal and dedicated attention to make your visit the best. It is a lovely romantic spot and there is just something about Cahernane that draws you back. A Spa is on the way as we go to press.

The Earls of Pembroke sure knew how to pick a location!

| 🐴 | 🐎 | 🖳 | ✏ | 🔪 | 🔌 | NET | H | P |

Owners:	The Browne Family
Address:	Muckross Road, Killarney, Co. Kerry.
Tel/Fax	064 31895/064 34340
No. Of Rooms	38
Price	
Double/Twin	€264
Single	€220
Family	€264
Dinner	Yes - Restaurant
Open	1st February – 30th November
Credit Cards	Visa MC Amex Diners Laser
Directions.	From Killarney Town follow the Kenmare Road for 1.5km. Hotel entrance is on the right.
Email:	info@cahernane.com
Web:	www.lucindaosullivan.com/cahernane

Carrig
Country House

CARAGH LAKE

Caragh Lake is a lush magnificent area
virtually hidden away from the Tourist be
they Irish or otherwise.   It has however
been a popular area for many years with
the Germans a number of whom bought
houses in the 1960's.

CARRIG COUNTRY HOUSE

We discovered Carrig Country House, an original 19th C.
hunting lodge, at Caragh Lake in 1997 quite by accident
when we arrived out there disheveled, distraught and
hungry, with two young boys on tow.   We were staying in a dreadful B.
& B. in Killorglin, which had thimbles of watery orange juice for
breakfast and brown psychedelic sheets from the 1970's and we nearly
cried when we realized we could have been in luxury in Carrig House
had we but known of it.   We couldn't find anywhere to eat and were at
one another's throats when a young girl told us about "the new house
out at the lake".   Off we took like the clappers, 4 miles out of Killorglin,
to find there was a God, and Heaven awaited in the shape of the
welcoming Frank Slattery, and his wife Mary, who had opened for
business that summer.   Even if we couldn't stay there on that occasion,
at least we were able to have dinner in the magnificent William Morris
papered diningroom overlooking the mysterious lake with its

mountainous background. We did however return again and it was as blissful as we had first thought. Arthur Rose Vincent chose Carrig House in which to live after his former residence, Muckross Estate in Killarney, was made over to the Irish State by his American father in law, following the death of his young wife. Arthur clearly had an eye for beauty. The 4 acres of gardens have 935 different species of mature trees and plants, including some very rare and exotic varieties, and are just divine. Dingly dell, mixes with rolling lawns sweeping down to the private jetty which has boats for fishing or just for guests' pleasure. Splendid new rooms have been added at Carrig including a Presidential Suite. The food is fabulous and Frank and Mary, while professional to their fingertips, are just fun. People relax and there is laughter and buzz at Carrig. We had torn ourselves reluctantly away and, as we drove out the gates, My Beloved surprisingly broke into verse "I come from haunts of coot and hern, I make a sudden sally..."

Owners:	Frank & Mary Slattery,
Address:	Caragh Lake, Killorglin, Co. Kerry.
Tel/Fax	066 9769100/066 9769166
No. Of Rooms	16
Price	
Suites	€230 - €375
Double/Twin	€130 - €220
Family	Extra bed in room €40 pp
Dinner	Yes
Open	Early March – Early December
Credit Cards	All Major Cards
Directions.	Left after 2.5 miles on N70 Killorglin-Glenbeigh Road (Ring of Kerry)
Email:	info@carrighouse.com
Web:	www.lucindaosullivan.com/carrighouse

Castlewood House

DINGLE

The Dingle peninsula is so intensely shatteringly beautiful that one can almost feel its raging tempestuous undercurrent churning away. The movie "Ryan's Daughter" brought people from all over the world to Dingle and they still come in their droves including one who has remained for some time - Fungi the dolphin, who is undoubtedly Dingle's most famous resident.

CASTLEWOOD HOUSE

Brian and Helen Heaton are a young couple who have brought their wealth of style, and experience at the upper end of the hospitality industry, into their spanking brand new Castlewood House, which has to be one of the finest Guest Houses I have ever been in.

Custom built to their very discerning specifications, Castlewood offers the guest the ultimate in luxury accommodation, the equivalent of any of the finest 5 star hotels, but of course at a fraction of 5 Star Hotel prices. Castlewood curves gently demi lune style overlooking Dingle Bay and all of the bedrooms have magnificent views of the water. Each bedroom is individually themed, an Oriental room, a French room, and so on - all equally gorgeous – for which Brian and Helen spent months buying here and abroad for all of the special little details. Each room also has a CD/DVD player, satellite TV, mini fridge,

Internet access, hospitality trays, and the lovely bathrooms have whirlpool baths and power showers.

From the moment you cross the doorstep into the wide elegant hall with curved staircase and double doors to the drawingroom and diningroom you realise it is magnificently furnished with beautiful antiques and paintings. The drawingroom is splendid, the diningroom lovely, you won't want to leave here. Helen has superb taste perhaps inherited from her mother, who is a distinguished Artist and some of her work can be seen on the walls of Castlewood.

You will enjoy breakfast overlooking the water. The buffet is lavish with a beautiful selection of fruits, cereals, cheeses, charcuterie, and scrumptious breads and pastries. The pancakes with a fruit topping and maple syrup are sinful as is Helen's creamed porridge with local organic honey or Bailey's. The delicious smoked salmon omelettes are another option – don't worry for the Full Irish is there too – Brian makes sure of that as well as a Fresh Fish of the Day option.

Brian and Helen are a charming and helpful young couple and will really add to the pleasure of your holiday.

Owners:	Brian and Helen Heaton
Address:	The Wood, Dingle, Co. Kerry.
Tel/Fax	066 9152788/066 9152110
No. Of Rooms	12
Price	
Double/Twin	€138
Single	€100
Family	€150
Dinner	No
Open	February to December
Credit Cards	Visa MC Diners Laser
Directions.	Located 500m from Dingle Town. Take main road towards Milltown, last house on right.
Email:	castlewoodhouse@eircom.net
Web:	www.lucindaosullivan.com/castlewooddingle

Glanleam Country House & Gardens

Glanleam House and estate is undoubtedly Paradise in Ireland for it is complete with its own Rain Forest – jungle. Situated on Valentia Island, (now linked to the mainland by a bridge), Glanleam House dates from the early 19th Century and was originally home to the Knight of Kerry. Magnificently and stylishly furnished to the very highest standard, blending the best of antique and modern furniture and design, it really is superb. The six bedrooms and one suite are cool and comfortable with beautiful views of the garden and water. Valentia is Europe's most westerly harbour with nothing but ocean between it and Newfoundland. The island also basks in the Gulf Stream climate and is an oasis of sub-tropical plants, ferns, myrtle, bamboos and the only remaining camphor tree in the British Isles. It was from Valentia Island that the first ever trans-Atlantic telegraph cable was laid and for years it was said there was better communication between Valentia and New York than Valentia and Dublin! In 1992 the oldest fossilized footprints in the northern hemisphere were discovered, nearly 400 million years old, and belonging to a marine tetrapod that pre-dated the dinosaurs. You needn't worry about dinosaurs, however, just enjoy the lovely rare Soay sheep and Connemara ponies living happily in this blissful haven. Dinner is available 5 nights a week with advance notice so do enquire on booking. Meta and her daughter, Jessica, are absolutely charming and they offer both Irish and German cuisine with fruit and vegetables from their own walled Victorian gardens. Superb local fresh fish, meat and poultry, feature and you can be assured that you will be admirably looked after at beautiful Glanleam. From here too you can arrange to visit the spectacular Skelligs Rocks. Deep sea, shore and lake fishing, watersports, hill walking and horseriding are all available locally. Golfers will find Waterville Golf Links an attraction.

Owners:	Meta & Jessica Kreissig
Address:	Glanleam Estate, Valentia Island, Co. Kerry.
Tel/Fax	066 9476176/ 066 9476108
No. Of Rooms	7
Price	
Double/Twin	€140 - €240 Low Season €170 - €300 Main Season
Dinner	Yes (Book in advance)
Open	March 17 – October 31
Credit Cards	Visa MC Amex
Directions.	Take R565 through Portmagee to Valentia Island. House signed.
Email:	info@glanleam.com
Web:	
www.lucindaosullivan.com/glanleam	

Gorman's Clifftop House

If you want to visit the most romantic setting, in one of the furthermost west establishment in Europe, you must stay at Gorman's Clifftop House at Glaise Bheag, near the small fishing village of Ballydavid, on the Slea Head Drive and Dingle Walking Way. The location has that absolute *aaaah* factor, for the stone fronted house faces out over Smerwick Harbour, Three Sisters Mountains, Sybil Head to the left, with the vastness of the Atlantic beyond. As if that is not enough, at the back of the house you have the spectacular vista of the Brandon Mountains

Vincent Gorman's family settled this wild and beautiful land in the 1700's but Sile only came to Dingle 25 years ago on holiday, met Vincent and fell in love, not only with him, but also with Dingle. They are the most welcoming and warm couple you could meet and you will have a brilliant time at their home.

The house is beautifully and sympathetically furnished to blend in with nature. Natural waxed pine mixes with the colours of the hedgerows and the beautiful pottery of Louis Mulcahy. Double rooms have kingsize beds whilst superior rooms have superking. There are direct dial phones, Internet access, TVs and all the amenities one could possibly want. Gorman's offer plenty of choice with room service available from 8 a.m. until 10 p.m. which is most unusual for this type of establishment.

Vincent and Sile are solicitous hosts and you will enjoy sitting around the cosy fire, sharing information, planning the next days trip, and meeting interesting people from all over the world. The diningroom faces the water and you can expect Vincent's delicious food to perhaps include crab claws with garlic butter, or traditional potato cakes with Annascaul black pudding, followed by juicy prawns or hoppingly fresh turbot, straight from the local fishing boats, served perhaps with vanilla and orange syrup with lentils. Do leave room for the chocolate cake, it is to die for.

There is nothing more magical than sitting out in Gorman's garden with a decent glass of wine listening to roar of the waves and watching the sun go down. It is a wonderful place, rejuvenating, fun, so good for the soul, and an experience you will never forget.

Owners:	Vincent & Sile Gorman
Address:	Glaise Bheag, Ballydavid, Dingle Peninsula, Co. Kerry.
Tel/Fax	066 9155162/066 9155003
No. Of Rooms	9
Price	
Double/Twin	€130 - €160
Single	€75 - €120
Family	€150 - €195
Dinner	Yes – Restaurant
Open	April – October
	November – March by advance reservation only
Credit Cards	Visa MC Laser
Directions.	Drive through Dingle, harbour on left to roundabout, Straight across – signposted "An Fheothanach" – 8 miles keep left but do not turn left.
Email:	info@gormans-clifftophouse.com
Web:	www.lucindaosullivan.com/gormansclifftop

Great Southern Hotel & Spa Killarney

The first time I was in Killarney was many years ago, with a gang of girls, for the Circuit of Ireland Rally. We weren't really interested in the Rally more in what was driving the cars! People congregated in the Bar in the Great Southern Hotel and I was mesmerized by how beautiful it was for we were staying in a B. & B. with pink nylon sheets and doubtful towels. That is all a long time ago.

The Great Southern Hotel is one of the Grand Old Ladies of the Irish hospitality scene and very recently she has not just had Botox but a major face lift returning her to the ranks she deserves as one of the finest Hotels in Ireland. Presidents and Princes have been entertained at the GSH Killarney and there is a very definite feeling of regal splendour from the moment you approach the impressive pillared entrance, go up the steps and know that you are somewhere special. The Hotel is fabulously located close to the old world Railway Station and, if you use your imagination a little, you can just see the Victorian ladies in hoop dresses alighting from the train and walking across to the Hotel with bearers in tow carrying stacks of trunks. Although the Hotel is in the centre of Killarney it is on 20 acres of secluded landscaped gardens in an amazing setting. The staff are delightful and will look after you admirably. The bedrooms are spacious and elegant with high ceilings and facilities for modem, fax and email along with a minibar, T.V. and radio. Luxury Suites have been individually designed

to re-create an old world ambience and some have chandeliers and separate dressing rooms. The two bedroomed Presidential and Ambassador suites are amazing. There are two dining options and I suggest you try them both. The Garden Restaurant is fabulous with its high domed ceiling and gracious ambience – just think of how much gold leaf was used to restore this room to its present magnificence. Peppers is the Hotel's more casual Bistro style Restaurant doing beautiful food in lovely surroundings. The Innisfallen Spa at the Southern has a wide range of facilities so that you can be totally pampered – try the Hydro-massage baths they are brilliant, followed by a Monsoon Shower. Apart from rates shown below, visit website for fantastic special offers.

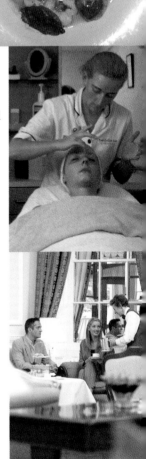

Owners:	Conor Hennigan (General Manager)
Address:	Town Centre, Killarney, Co. Kerry.
Tel/Fax	064 38000/064 31642
No. Of Rooms	172
Price	
Double	€260
Twin	€260
Single	€260
Family	€260
Dinner	Yes – 2 Restaurants
Open	All Year
Credit Cards	All Major Cards
Directions.	Located on the Square in Killarney Town
Email:	res@killarney-gsh.com
Web:	www.lucindaosullivan.com/gshkillarney

NET P

Great Southern Hotel Parknasilla

PARKNASILLA

I always insist that we set off a day in advance when we are going to the Great Southern at Parknasilla because, I just love it so much I want to arrive in a civilized state, and not be below par for one minute. We break the back of the journey by staying somewhere reasonably priced and reasonably close. Next morning refreshed and ready to make our entrance we take a leisurely drive out through Cahirciveen, around the Ring of Kerry, absolutely revelling in just being alive, and being in the spectacular scenery that is the Ring of Kerry. Brave souls, and we were those soldiers one year, can drive from Caragh Lake out over the McGillicuddy Reeks, past mountainy rangy goats and hair-raising roads, emerging down close to Sneem.

GREAT SOUTHERN HOTEL PARKNASILLA

The Great Southern Hotel at Parknasilla is the jewel in the crown of the Great Southern Hotel Group, sitting majestically in 300 acres of the most beautiful lush sub-tropical parkland overlooking Kenmare Bay.

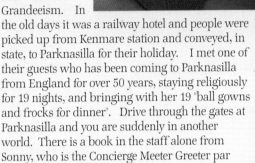

It is probably the most splendid Hotel in the country, in the sense of location and Victorian Grandeeism. In the old days it was a railway hotel and people were picked up from Kenmare station and conveyed, in state, to Parknasilla for their holiday. I met one of their guests who has been coming to Parknasilla from England for over 50 years, staying religiously for 19 nights, and bringing with her 19 "ball gowns and frocks for dinner". Drive through the gates at Parknasilla and you are suddenly in another world. There is a book in the staff alone from Sonny, who is the Concierge Meeter Greeter par extraordinaire to beat all par extraordinaires, to Head Porter Michael and Jackie the Maitre d' of the dining room. These are the smoothest most accomplished men at their trades that you are likely to meet anywhere in the world – Masters at their Arts – who greet you as though you were the most important person ever, a long lost friend, and will look after you likewise. The bedrooms are spacious and comfortable and for me a great switch off point. Look out front and people will be sitting around on the terrace sipping cool drinks or walking the grounds. There is a 12 Hole Golf Course, Horse riding, boat trips around the rugged inlets on the Parknasilla Princess. The dining room is vast and yet the food does not suffer from its size. Retire to the Library, view the wonderful art collection, swim in the pool, luxuriate in the Canadian Outdoor Hot tub, take part in the walks or activities organized, get totally tiddily, dance the mambo after dinner to the band, nobody will bat an eyelid! It's wonderful. Visit website for fantastic special offers.

Owners:	Patrick Cussen (General Manager)
Address:	Parknasilla, Sneem, Co. Kerry.
Tel/Fax	064 45122/064 45323
No. Of Rooms	83
Price	
Double	€260
Twin	€260
Single	€260
Family	€260
Dinner	Yes
Open	All Year
Credit Cards	All Major Cards
Directions.	N70 from Kenmare, Estate entrance after Tahilla just before Sneem Village.
Email:	res@parknasilla-gsh.com
Web:	www.lucindaosullivan.com/gshparknasilla

Heaton's Guesthouse

We had intended setting off for Dingle early in the morning but we fell by the wayside. We had stayed at a house up at Caragh Lake, demurely had dinner beside an American couple without exchanging a word, walked around the house and came back in to the drawingroom to sit quietly in a bay window. Suddenly the door opened and a bright smiling blonde girl came in sat down and introduced herself as Marian. She and her husband, Nigel, were on their first trip to Ireland as their son was on a school rugby trip in Limerick. As often happens with English people who have no family connections with Ireland, it was their first trip here, and frankly they wouldn't have come unless they had to, for they usually went to exotic locations. We had a drink, and another drink before Nigel sensibly suggested they retire. Next morning at breakfast we all waved at one another, had little polite chats, and nodded to the Americans. We got our bags out to the car where the American couple were trying to map out their route. Telling us they had Restaurants in the States, I confessed to being probably their archenemy – a Restaurant Critic. With that a German car swung into the car park and came over to join in. On learning my occupation the German went to his car boot and took out a little fold up table, spread a check cloth, took out two bottles of wine from his region in Germany, some titbits, special knives and told us he had been coming to Ireland for over 30 years, using the same table, knives and equipment each year! Nigel and Marian emerged and we had the League of Nations Irish, English, Americans and Germans, having a party in a Car park in Kerry, They had never experienced anything like it and told us since it was the best trip of their lives. That's what Kerry and Ireland is really all about.

HEATON'S GUESTHOUSE

Cameron and Nuala Heaton's eponymous Guesthouse is spectacularly located on the edge of the water with magnificent views of Dingle Bay. There is something special about being close to the water that is infectious and life giving. The shimmering ripples are wonderful to sit by during the summer and stunningly dramatic viewed through a window in the depths of winter. Heaton's has 16 rooms, standard, deluxe and Junior Suites, take your choice, but all are beautifully draped and furnished in cool clear, up to the minute, stylish colours. Each with T.V. Tea/Coffee makers, and superb bathrooms with power-showers, are spacious and have everything you could possibly want for your comfort. There is a large foyer and a lounge sittingroom area with big comfortable sofas where you can snuggle up, cosy up, or just relax. Breakfast is served in the diningroom which also makes the most of the magnificent views with big plate glass windows. This is daughter, Jackie's, area and you can chose from an amazing selection which includes juices, fruits, cereals, stewed fruits – rhubarb or apple- porridge with a dram of Drambuie, brown sugar and cream, followed by the traditional Irish, or Catch of the day, local Smoked Salmon and scrambled egg. Preserves and breads are home-made. Children over 8 welcome. Cameron and Nuala are delightful people, as is their daughter Jackie, and superb hospitality is their middle name.

Owners:	Cameron & Nuala Heaton
Address:	The Wood, Dingle, Co. Kerry.
Tel/Fax	066 9152288/066 9152324
No. Of Rooms	16
Price	
Junior Suite	€180
Double/Twin	€130
Single	€95
Family	€160
Dinner	No
Open	February 6 – January 2
Credit Cards	Visa MC
Directions.	Look for Marina – Heaton's is about 600m beyond it.
Email:	heatons@iol.ie
Web:	www.lucindaosullivan.com/heatons

Loch Lein
Country House Hotel

There wouldn't be a Killarney without the famous Lakes and, whether you go to Killarney to see them, or to take a trip around the Muckross Estate by jaunting car, or just for the craic, it is certainly a bonus to be based in a lovely Country House right on the lakeshore. Loch Lein Country House is a superb small hotel overlooking the famous lower lake, after which the house is called.

"This is a gem of a location", we thought, on discovering it. Imagine what a top movie star or golfer would pay for this exclusive privacy and serenity but, no, we discovered Loch Lein Country House was open to everyone. The wide spacious tiled entrance hall with curving staircase and potted palms gives an inkling of the cool calm beautifully appointed bedrooms. Lake View Bedrooms are slightly more expensive but all are very nice and dinner is available in the hotel's Legends Restaurant overlooking the water. Modern Irish food is on the menu - roast collops of monkfish on leek and bacon mash, or maybe wild salmon, Barbary duck with summer fruit compote or a good steak with red wine jus followed by scrumptious puddings. You can relax in the

drawing room with a nightcap from the bar and plan tomorrow's trip or walk off the calories!

Close to four 18-hole Championship Golf Courses, Loch Lein also has the facility of a putting green and a drying room. The very friendly hosts, Paul and Annette Corridan, will arrange transport for you or tailor your itinerary, as well as provide early breakfasts or brunch. It is also an angler's paradise with salmon and trout fishing on the Lakes of Killarney, the Rivers Flesk and Laune. Fishing is free on the Killarney Lakes (except Kilbrean). Permits are needed for fishing the rivers and a licence is needed for salmon fishing. Rowing boats are available for hire locally, with or without a boatman, and all weather cruises depart Ross Castle on a regular basis. This is a wonderful area too if you are a walker – think of the glorious parklands and the lakeshore to explore.

One thing you can really be sure of is personal service and attention from the Corridan family on your trip.

Owners:	Paul & Annette Corridan,
Address:	Old Golf Course Road, Fossa, Killarney. Co. Kerry.
Tel/Fax	064 31260/064 36151
No. Of Rooms	25
Double/Twin	Superior `€110 - €140. Lake View €130 - €170
Single	€75 - €95
Family	€160 - €200
Dinner	Yes - Restaurant
Open	1st April – 2nd November
Credit Cards	Visa MC Laser
Directions.	Take N72 W from Killarney. In Village of Fossa take immediate turn left after Church.
Email:	stay@lochlein.com
Web:	www.lucindaosullivan.com/lochlein

Manor West Hotel Spa
& Leisure Club

On the outskirts of Tralee, on the Killarney Road, stands the spanking new Manor West Hotel. Custom built from the ground up, this fine addition to Tralee offers contemporary 4 star comfort and service under the eagle eye of one of the best Hoteliers in the Country, General Manager Jim Feeney, who for many years oversaw the smooth running of the Great Southern Hotel at Parknasilla.

Your arrival in the cool marble spacious lobby with its magnificent paintings and prestigious and stylish lounge area leaves you in no doubt as to the good things to come. Manor West boasts 77 rooms with all the goodies one expects of a modern day hotel and there are also 10 suites on the top floor, Master, Executive or Junior, where you can either relax, or work, in the utmost luxury.

Off the spacious lobby is the Hotel's modern restaurant, The Walnut Room. Stylishly designed and buzzing with atmosphere, right in the centre is what might be called the "inner circle" two half moon sections facing one another which would make a great set for a movie. It is a lovely room and you can expect to dine on the best of Kerry produce. If you want to eat more informally there is the option of the very casual style Mercantile Bar with its flat screen TVs and self-service food area.

Manor West is ideal too for families who will love the Leisure Club facilities. There is an 18 metre swimming pool, sauna, steam room, Jacuzzi and a state of the art gymnasium. Whilst Dad is taking the kids to the pool, this is the time you can take yourself off to the Harmony Spa which has 5 treatment rooms, Laconium, Razul and Aroma Steam Room. Treat yourself to a body wrap and then take yourself off to spend his money at the nearby shopping centre! He won't know you by the time you come back!

The Hotel's easy parking and proximity to the busy commercial town of Tralee makes it an ideal base for the businessman. While, it's central location in the beautiful Kingdom of Kerry makes it the perfect base for the tourist who wishes to explore the delights of this splendid County.

Kerry is the Kingdom.

Owners:	Jim Feeney (General Manager)
Address:	Killarney Road, Tralee, Co. Kerry.
Tel/Fax	066 7194500/066 7194522
No. Of Rooms	77
Price	
Suites	From €160
Double/Twin	From €120
Single	From € 85
Family	From €180
Dinner	Yes – 2 Restaurants
Open	All Year
Credit Cards	Visa MC Amex Laser
Directions.	Situated on the N22 – Main Limerick/Killarney Road into Tralee Town
Email:	info@manorwesthotel.ie
Web:	www.lucindaosullivan.com/manorwest

NET P

Meadowlands Hotel

"Meadowlands"? Repeated the telephone enquiry operator. "Yes", I said, "its an Hotel in Tralee". "I know", she said, "I was there last night and the food is gorgeous". Now, it wasn't the "pale moon shining" nor the fabled Rose that drew me to Tralee. Word had filtered through that the owners of Meadowlands, Padraig and Peigi O'Mathuna, were in the fish business in Dingle, "had their own trawlers", and consequently the Hotel Restaurant, "An Pota Stoir" was specializing, in beautiful fresh seafood. It was true and the whisper in the breeze was right!

The first thing that struck us about the rose coloured hotel was its spaciousness and lots of parking. The corridors are wide and the bedrooms bigger than average and very nicely decorated – beautiful heavily lined beige silk curtains, nice lamps, and furnishings and very comfortable beds. The bathrooms are very pretty, with floral painted walls, good fittings and pretty New England style doors with glass windowpanes discreetly covered with net. We came down to the Johnny Franks Bar, which is clearly very popular with local people. Modern "Traditional Irish," I suppose is how you might describe it, with a faux library at the upper level and high ceilings, lots of wood and it also does excellent barfood. The split level Pota Stoir Restaurant is casual in ethos, with lots of pine, brick, wall lights and so on, but the food and service is far from casual. There was a relaxed atmosphere as the lady pianist played away all the old favourites which lent a lovely ambience of real Ireland.

Young local man John O'Leary is the Head Chef and is clearly innovative and dedicated. You can expect to see creamy Dingle Bay seafood chowder or maybe tian of Maharees crabmeat wrapped around by a ribbon of sweet marinated cucumber and topped with shredded deep fried onion ... and the scallops with Annascaul black pudding. yum ... or the panfried fillets of turbot fit ...for a prince.

 NET P

Meadowlands is in a great location in Tralee, the gateway to Dingle, so you can take trips either up to Clare or further south around Kerry – a great central base.

Now you know where to bring your Rose for a bit of craic in Johnny Franks and good food in an Pota Stoir ...

Owners:	Padraig and Peigi O'Mathuna
Address:	Oakpark, Tralee, Co. Kerry.
Tel/Fax	066 7180444/0667180964
No. Of Rooms	58
Price	
Suite	€250 - € 350
Double/Twin	€180
Single	€80
Family	€20 pp supplement for Executive Room
Dinner	Restaurant & Bar food
Open	All Year
Credit Cards	Visa MC Amex Laser
Directions.	The Hotel is situated on the N69, the Listowel Road.
Email:	info@meadowlandshotel.com
Web:	www.lucindaosullivan.com/meadowlands

135

Muckross Park Hotel & Spa

Jackie Lavin and Bill Cullen are one of Ireland's celebrity couples. Kerry born Jackie, is long recognised as one of Ireland's beauties, as well as being an astute business woman, and Dublin born Bill Cullen wrote his incredible life story *It's a Long Way from Penny Apples*, the royalties of which book, with his usual panache, Bill donated to the Irish Youth Foundation.

Some years ago Jackie and Bill bought the Muckross Park Hotel uniquely located in the National Park on the Lakes of Killarney. A hotel since 1795 and originally part of the Muckross Estate owned by the Herbert family, it has seen visitors as diverse as Michael Collins, the Liberator Daniel O'Connell and Queen Victoria. The Muckross Park Hotel was the haunt too of great writers, its informal Bistro "GB Shaw's" is named after George Bernard Shaw, who loved to stay with his wife, Charlotte Payne Townsend and, the new Atrium has hand painted wall inscriptions by W.B. Yeats and by the contemporary Irish poet, Brendan Kennelly.

Now a 5 star hotel, there is a glorious olde world luxurious spaciousness to the entrance hall and gracious Country House reception rooms in the original house. The Piano Lounge – a perfect Victorian drawingroom - with its grand piano, magnificent sofas, beautiful fabrics, antiques and chandeliers is an oasis of calm. The Blue Pool Restaurant offers a fine dining experience whilst the bedrooms are havens of peace. I love too the little olde worlde garden just across the road.

However, the Muckross Park Hotel is not all about history for the facilities are second to none. "Molly Darcy's", their traditional Irish bar

with stonewalls, wooden floors, beamed ceilings and open fires, has a great atmosphere and does excellent food virtually all day. The attentive staff were really on the ball which is always a sign of great management. On top of this a major development plan has seen the addition of forty new superior bedrooms including four executive suites bringing the number of rooms to 108 along with the addition of a sublime new Luxury Health Spa with ten treatment rooms. Oh bliss.

So, you see, the craic is mighty, the five star facilities second to none, and now you can also pamper yourself in the magnificent Spa as part of your historical trip to Killarney.

Owners:	Jackie Lavin & Bill Cullen
Address	Muckross Village, Lakes of Killarney, Co. Kerry.
Tel/Fax	064 31938/064 31965
No. Of Rooms	108
Price	
Double/Twin	€300 - €500
Single	€150 - €280
Family	€300 - €500
Dinner	Yes – 2 Restaurants + Bar Food
Open	All Year
Credit Cards	Visa MC Amex Diners Laser
Directions.	Take the Muckross Road to the National Park. Past Muckross Village on the left hand side. Adjacent to Muckross House & Gardens.
Email:	info@muckrosspark.com
Web:	www.lucindaosullivan.com/muckrosspark

Muxnaw Lodge

There is a wide variety of accommodation and high prices in Kenmare so finding that something in between can sometimes be difficult but I found just the place.

Muxnaw Lodge is a lovely gabled house, a former Hunting Lodge built in 1801 ideally situated very close to the town on the Castletownbere Road. Muxnaw is a homely but understatedly classy establishment nestled on 3 acres of fine gardens, complete with its own all weather tennis court, and enjoying outstanding views of the Kenmare River and suspension bridge. Tranquil bedrooms are all different, furnished with beautiful antiques and all have tea and coffee making facilities. Its success is a credit to the wonderful hospitality of its hostess, Hannah Boland, as well as the comforts provided. Hannah knows the area like the back of her hand and delights in mapping out routes and setting her guests off on the proper track for the day. I have indeed seen her spend many an afternoon, after she has served the most delectable afternoon tea, chatting with her guests and pouring over maps and routes, planning the remainder of their holiday.

Kenmare has any number of restaurants to tickle one's taste buds and Hannah will mark your card as to which are the best and most suitable for you. You can leave the car at Muxnaw and just stroll down the town without wondering whether you have to worry about having that second drink before you drive home. Dinner is available with advance notice and beautiful salmon cooked in the big Aga cooker is one of Hannah's specialities. There is no wine licence so you are more than welcome to bring your own. Breakfast is superb, juices, fruit, and cereals with delicious breads and followed by eggs any way you

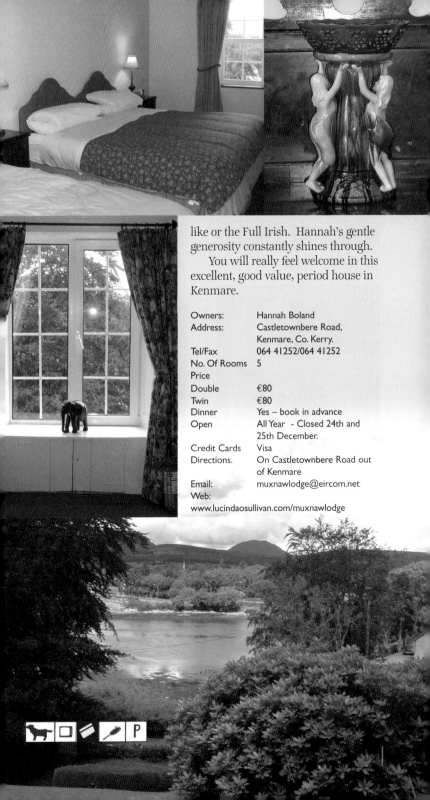

like or the Full Irish. Hannah's gentle generosity constantly shines through.

You will really feel welcome in this excellent, good value, period house in Kenmare.

Owners:	Hannah Boland
Address:	Castletownbere Road, Kenmare, Co. Kerry.
Tel/Fax	064 41252/064 41252
No. Of Rooms	5
Price	
Double	€80
Twin	€80
Dinner	Yes – book in advance
Open	All Year - Closed 24th and 25th December.
Credit Cards	Visa
Directions.	On Castletownbere Road out of Kenmare
Email:	muxnawlodge@eircom.net
Web:	
www.lucindaosullivan.com/muxnawlodge	

County Kilkenny

Kilkenny is a county of rich farmland, quaint villages and towns, well endowed with mediaeval ruins and friendly people who are not reluctant to talk about hurling, the very special Gaelic game at which Kilkenny people excel. Kilkenny City, on the River Nore, is a bustling busy place defined by the magnificent Kilkenny Castle, former home to the Butlers of Ormonde. The City has many hotels, guesthouses and bars and is very popular now for weekend breaks and for stag and hen parties. The surrounding county is not short on items of historical interest like Kilcree Round Tower, Jerpoint Abbey, and the ruin of Kells Priory. Go to Graiguenamanagh on the River Barrow, the home of Duiske Abbey, founded in 1204, and although much altered over the years the 13th Century interior has been lovingly preserved. Bennettsbridge, an area now home to many craft industries such as the Nicholas Mosse Pottery, is worth a visit, as is Thomastown, just north of Jerpoint, formerly a walled town of some importance, and close to the magnificent Championship Golf Course of Mount Juliet. Relax with a glass of Guinness, or whatever, in the tree lined square, or by the river, of interesting Inistioque, which is overlooked by the ruin of the Woodstock Estate, burned down in 1922. Kilkenny is a fabulous county.

"I have made an important discovery...that alcohol, taken in sufficient quantities, produces all the effects of intoxication".
(OSCAR WILDE)

Lacken House

Well, I guess I am kind of biased when it comes to Lacken House because my father lived there as a child so it, and Kilkenny City, have a tremendous sentimental attachment for me. In fact it's a bit like a magnet, I can't stay away from the Marble City and County.

Kilkenny is Ireland's finest medieval city. There is just so much to do and see. The Castle, which dominates and creates a magical atmosphere, is a "must see" for all visitors – the silk lined walls, furnishings and paintings are glorious. The other "must see" is the 13th C. St. Canice's Cathedral. Nowadays Kilkenny is a hopping vibrant place and very popular for weekend breaks. There are lots of pubs, restaurants, hotels, galleries and shops but the trick is to find that Great Place to Stay with individual attention and good food1.

Lacken House is a lovely Victorian house, built as a Dower House in 1847 for Viscount Montmorency. It was taken over recently by a young husband and wife team, Trevor Toner and Jackie Kennedy Toner, who have transformed it into a superb Guesthouse. Food is a feature at Lacken House so book dinner when making your reservation. Having secured your place at the table, you can then turn your thoughts perhaps to pan seared foie gras wrapped in duck magret served with caramelised banana and truffled honey or, you might fancy starting with panfried hake on squid ink risotto with sautéed scallop and clams. When you have whetted your appetite on either of those you can concentrate on the main courses which might include tender fillet of beef with spinach and celeriac, poached oyster, wholegrain mustard and Guinness reduction but there will be a wide choice and an excellent

wine list. After that lot you can retire to the drawingroom for a nightcap by the blazing fire before cosying up in the delightful bedrooms, which have been totally revamped by Trevor and Jackie, all now having big beds, beautiful Italian fabric wallpapers, luxury Wilton carpets and everything else one might want.

Also available in-room (book in advance) are Holistic Massage Treatments by a registered practitioner – so pamper yourself if he disappears to play golf.

Lacken House is the perfect place for that perfect break in perfectly beautiful Kilkenny

Owners:	Trevor and Jackie Kennedy Toner
Address:	Dublin Road, Kilkenny City, Co. Kilkenny.
Tel/Fax	056 7761085/056 7762435
No. Of Rooms	10
Price	
Double/Twin	€150
Family	€200 (up to 3 children sharing)
Dinner	Restaurant
Open	All Year – Closed 24th – 27th December
Credit Cards	Visa MC Amex Laser
Directions.	Located on N10 in Kilkenny City on main Dublin/Carlow Road.
Email:	info@lackenhouse.ie
Web:	www.lucindaosullivan.com/lackenhouse

Mount Juliet Conrad

Mount Juliet is a magnificent Georgian Mansion built by the Earl of Carrick, overlooking the River Nore, on 1500 acres of unspoiled woodland and meandering waters in Thomastown, South Kilkenny.   Latterly, Mount Juliet was owned by the late Major Victor McCalmont and his wife Bunty, well known figures on the Irish social scene.   Hunting, shootin', fishin', House Parties, were the thing along, with the Dublin Horse Show, Hacking Jackets from Callaghan's of Dame Street, antiques from Louis Wine.   The lives of staff in those days revolved around the big Estate and very often went from generation to generation of minding "the Major" and previous incumbents.   Mount Juliet was developed with great foresight and subtlety by businessman, Tim Mahony, for even though you drive through the Jack Nicklaus designed 18 hole Championship Golf Course, past the self catering Rose Garden Lodges and Hunters Yard complex, the house is far enough away to retain the illusion of being on a private estate and still feels more "Country House" than Hotel.   Now part of the Conrad Hotel Group, if your days aren't filled with golf or country pursuits, you can chill out and be pampered at the Health Club and Spa. There are two Restaurants, the Lady Helen Diningroom, with really superb food.   Albert Roux the famous French Chef comes to Mount Juliet to shoot and he cooked the favourite

soufflé of the late Queen Mother for us. The other dining option is Kendals Restaurant in the Hunters Yard which is large and buzzy. The rooms in the main house are gracious and beautiful and the modern rooms in the Hunters yard are super. Breakfast in the Lady Helen Room overlooking the River, rolling acres and romping young cattle, is simply bliss with a tremendous circular array of fresh, dried and exotic fruits, pastries, French yoghurts, cheeses, cold cuts, smoothies, porridge with fresh cream or honey, pancakes with maple syrup, cinnamon sugar and Wexford strawberries. "Would you like to try Tiger's Breakfast"? Asked the Restaurant Manager. I was still romancing about the classy Colonial days, Indiaaah and all that, forgetting that more recent blow in, Tiger Woods, until I was enlightened. Anyway, Tiger's breakfast is stacked French toast and smoked salmon topped with poached eggs. You might fancy "The Major's breakfast" which delves into the nether regions of liver and kidneys- strong stuff first thing. Mount Juliet is a glorious place, it is not just the house and nice staff, but the lushness of the grounds and winding paths which are a constant reminder of another life – people crave peace and space they will find it all here. Best rates available online at www.conradhotels.com. It is one of the finest Country Estates in Ireland.

Owners:	Antony Treston (General Manager)
Address:	Thomastown, Co. Kilkenny.
Tel/Fax	056 7773000/056 7773019
No. Of Rooms	58
Price	
Double/Twin	From €179
Single	From €162
Family	From €350 – Rose Garden Lodge
Dinner	Yes – 2 Restaurants
Open	All Year
Credit Cards	All Major Cards
Directions.	Follow signs from Thomastown
Email:	mountjulietinfo@conradhotels.com
Web:	www.lucindaosullivan.com/mountjuliet

18h	NET	H	P	

County Laois

Laois is a very unassuming and modest county, which does little to blow its own trumpet but does have its share of interesting history. For example, the county's principal town of Portlaoise was originally named Maryborough after Mary Tudor of Britain. It is a thriving business town and site of the Republic's main prison, which has housed many of the political prisoners during the recent "troubles". Ten miles south of Portlaoise is Abbeyleix, named after a Cistercian Abbey founded there in 1183 but the village was vastly altered in the 18th century by the Viscount De Vesci whose descendants resided there until very recently. Stradbally is well known for its Steam Museum and its narrow gauge railway where a 19th century steam locomotive, formerly used in the Guinness Brewery, runs about six times a year. If you are driving beware of your speed when approaching Cullahill on your way south for I have sad memories of being caught in a speed trap there, and me in reverse!

"Modesty is the art of encouraging people to find out for themselves
how wonderful you are"
(ANON)

Preston House

When I was a child we used stay near Abbeyleix, as my Uncle was a Curate of the Parish, so I knew the area pretty well. That was in the days when Earl and Countess de Vesci lived in Abbeyleix in the big estate. There is always something about a town that has the remnants of auld decency about it. I had a Siamese cat whose name was Suzuki San who was entered in the local Agricultural Show - she was a rare sight in a midland town then. Suzi won second prize, which didn't qualify for a ribbon, and I felt so hurt for her - home we went in Uncle's car and out came the blue ribbon and the biggest bestest rosette ever ensued. Abbeyleix has an excellent heritage centre but for heritage of another sort drop into Morrissey's Bar.

PRESTON HOUSE

Alison and Michael Dowling's Preston House, on the main street in Abbeyleix, is quite rightly admired and lauded by everyone who ever visits there, be it just for lunch or dinner passing through, or staying overnight. The fine Georgian creeper clad former schoolhouse is delightfully warm and welcoming. Walk through the door and you will be assailed with appetizing aromas from the kitchen, which is always a good omen. There is a tremendous buzz as people pour in for Alison's wonderful food - wholesome, fresh, thoughtful and innovative - just as she is herself a no nonsense person with a tremendous warmth and friendliness. Here, at lunchtime, you will see the local Bank Manager, Parish Priest or Doctor, unable to resist what is going to be on Alison's menu today, but you definitely need to get in early for a table in this lovely Restaurant which is straight out of Country Life. Dense pungent smoked haddock chowder is legendary as is the chicken liver pate. Mainers might include salmon with hollandaise or a fine fillet of cod cooked to perfection and served with a lemon butter sauce accompanied by wholesome fresh vegetables and wonderful potatoes. Dinner is wonderful, with an excellent selection of wines, and all you have to do

after dining lavishly is toddle upstairs, no driving, and look forward to yet more wonderful food at breakfast. The bedrooms are great, full of atmosphere, with big comfortable beds, beautiful crisp bedlinen, T.V.'s, magazines, sofas, and pine floors scattered with rugs, all the comforts you expect in a lovely country house. Preston House is a stress free offering comfort and divine home cooked food from a country loving family.

Owners:	Michael and Alison Dowling
Address:	Abbeyleix, Co. Laois.
Tel/Fax	0502 31432/0502 31432
No. Of Rooms	4
Price	
Double/Twin	From €120
Single	From €70
Dinner	Yes - Restaurant
Open	All Year except Christmas
Credit Cards	Visa MC
Directions.	On the Cork side on Abbeyleix Town
Email:	prestonhouse@eircom.net
Web:	www.lucindaosullivan.com/prestonhouse

County Limerick

Limerick City, located at the lowest fording point of the River Shannon, is sports mad whether it be Gaelic football, hurling, horse racing, soccer or particularly rugby football which boasts that well known Limerick invention the "Garryowen":- the high kick forward which allows your team to charge after it and put the fear of God into the poor player who happens to be trying to catch it. It is also famous as the location of Frank McCourt's book *Angela's Ashes*, although some of its inhabitants find it hard to

accept. From the time the Vikings sailed up the Shannon and settled there, the place has had a troubled history but it is probably best remembered for the Williamite Siege in the late 1600's resisted by the Irish, led by Patrick Sarsfield.   Probably the best-known tourist attraction in the city is the Hunt Museum, which has a collection to rival Dublin's National Gallery. In the late 1930's and early 1940's, Foynes was the terminus for the transatlantic Flying Boat service, and is home now to a Flying Boat Museum. Kilmallock and its nearby Museum is only four miles from Bruree, whose claim to fame is that it was the childhood home of Eamonn de Valera, former prominent 1916 figure, Taoiseach, and President of Ireland. The gem in the county's crown is the beautiful picturesque village of Adare which has many up market fine antique shops, friendly pubs, excellent Restaurants and
art shops but also has a number of beautifully maintained
thatched cottages and is regarded as the prettiest village in
Ireland.

"The one duty we have to history is to re-write it"
(OSCAR WILDE)

Dunraven Arms Hotel

Every November I look forward to an Invitation from my Horsey friends to The Hunt Ball in Adare. Whilst a night of Tallyho with The Equine Fraternity of Limerick has its own special appeal, the real appeal for His Nibs and myself is to escape to Irelands prettiest village and stay in The Dunraven Arms, which never disappoints. This year was no exception and, even though it was a bleak mid winter day when we descended on Adare, the village looked stunning with its many thatched cottages, up market restaurants, funky art galleries, and serious Antique Shops. The Dunraven Arms with its richly painted walls and limestone trims stands out like a beacon of light and welcome in Adare Built in 1792, The Dunraven Arms is wonderfully stylish and one is always assured of a warm welcome. We arrived in the early afternoon in time for a swim in the leisure centre and for me a facial. Our rooms were beautifully furnished and filled with every creature comfort, Bliss. Suites and Junior Suites are superb with ample seating areas and dressing rooms. I have had many an encounter with shoddy service delivered by souls that possess what I call "The After the Party Look", not

so in Dunraven Arms. There was an abundance of extremely well groomed, well trained and very helpful staff to cater to our every whim. On the morning after, when we trundled down to breakfast, many of us bearing the aforementioned "After The Party Look" there was a feast of freshly squeezed juices of all types, platters of fruit, bowls of cereals, steaming hot silver pots of tea, and lovely breads but, best of all, hidden under a silver dome was the most delicious baked ham which is their Sunday morning speciality. From all my friends who have stayed in the Dunraven Arms I have never heard anything but high praise and, I can guarantee you that I would walk barefoot on broken glass back to The Dunraven Arms just for a sliver of that honey baked ham. The food is wonderful, the service is excellent, and the location is stunning. Golly gosh old boy, an all round corker!

Owners:	Louis Murphy
Address:	Adare, Co. Limerick.
Tel/Fax	061 396633/061 396541
No. Of Rooms	74
Price	
Suite/Junior Suite	€338 - €422 + 12.5% Service Charge
Double/Twin	From €220 + 12.5% Service Charge
Single	From €175 + 12.5% Service Charge
Family	On request
Dinner	Yes – 2 Restaurants
Open	All Year
Credit Cards	All Major Cards
Directions.	On right as you enter Adare Village from N21 from Limerick direction.
Email:	reservations@dunravenhotel.com
Web:	www.lucindaosullivan.com/dunravenarms

County Longford

Bordered by Ireland's greatest river, the Shannon in the west and counties Westmeath and Cavan in the east, Longford is a quiet peaceful midland county with pleasant rolling countryside. It is reckoned that Pallas, 10 miles north of Glasson, is the birthplace of Oliver Goldsmith, author of "She Stoops to Conquer" and "The Vicar of Wakefield".

Longford Town is a large busy rambling place and home of St. Mel's Cathedral – and a pleasant restful spot. For the tourist interested in archaeology a visit to Corlea Trackway Visitor Centre (April – September), nine miles south of Longford is well worthwhile.

Three miles northeast of the Town is Carriglass Manor with its gardens and Costume Museum, open to the public from May to September. Carriglass was built in 1837, by Thomas Lefroy, who was probably the model for Mr. Darcy in "Pride and Prejudice" as, at one stage, he and Jane Austen were romantically involved. The house is still owned by the Lefroy family.

"The very essence of romance is uncertainty. If ever I get married, I'll certainly try to forget the fact."

(OSCAR WILDE)

Viewmount House

I went with a friend on a skite up to Co. Leitrim a couple of years ago to investigate a French Restaurant in the pretty village of Dromahair. It seemed quite extraordinary to find this large purpose built Restaurant in a fairly remote part of Ireland but we enjoyed it thoroughly.

On our way back to Dublin, we spotted Viewmount, an absolutely beautiful house built in 1740 by the Cuffe family. Viewmount was inherited by Thomas Packenham (first Baron of Longford) when he married Elizabeth Cuffe for, "What's your is mine" was the rule of thumb when husbands took a wife in those days. Viewmount has had various distinguished residents and in the late 19th Century was occupied by Harry McCann a famed gardener. James and Beryl Kearney have continued the gardening tradition for the house today sits on four acres of magnificent gardens, which are "supervised" by Oisin the friendly Irish Wolfhound. Stroll with Oisin amongst the large old trees, hedges, stone walls and orchard, the knot garden, herbaceous borders, Japanese garden, the blue grey garden or white garden, it is sublime. From the splendid red hall with open fire, a fine elegant staircase spirals up to big beautiful bedrooms very stylishly decorated and furnished with antiques, big beds, and rugs. The purple room is divine. From the bedrooms too there are serene views over the garden and the adjoining Longford Golf Club. Breakfast is served in the fabulous vaulted diningroom and includes fruits and muesli, pancakes with maple syrup and pecan nuts, or scrambled eggs with smoked salmon... After that you can visit the exquisite Belvedere House where Robert Rochfort imprisoned his wife, Mary Molesworth, for 31 years and also see Ireland's largest man made folly – The Jealous Wall. Nearby too is the beautiful Strokestown House with its famine museum. There is a lot of

fishing about on Lough Gowna, Lough Ree and the River Shannon. Just recently opened at Viewmount is their new Restaurant which is a wonderful addition because you will just be able to forget about the car, relax and enjoy a delicious meal without worrying about driving home after a glass or ten of wine.

Viewmount is a delightful house to visit for a break or ideal for stopping over on the way to Donegal or the far West and James and Beryl are very friendly with a great sense of humour...you will enjoy the place.

Owners:	James and Beryl Kearney
Address:	Dublin Road, Longford, Co. Longford.
Tel/Fax	043 41919/043 42906
No. Of Rooms	6
Price	
Suite	€120 - €160
Double/Twin	€90 - €110
Family	€90 - €110 + Children sharing half price
Dinner	Yes - Restaurant
Open	All Year
Credit Cards	Visa MC Amex
Directions.	On Dublin Road out of Longford
Email:	info@viewmounthouse.com
Web:	www.lucindaosullivan.com/viewmount

"No great artist ever sees things as they really are.
If he did, he would cease to be an artist."
(OSCAR WILDE)

County Mayo

Mayo is a beautiful county with a landscape of high cliffs, lonely mountains and fuchsia hedges and is renowned as the home of Grace O'Malley, the notorious female pirate, rustler, and rebel whose story is a book in itself. Grace's stronghold was at Clew Bay, which is close to the Pilgrim Mountain of Croagh Patrick, the highest mountain in the area. It is from this spot that Ireland's patron Saint is said to have rid the country of snakes. Off to the east, situated snugly between Lough Conn and Lough Cullin is Pontoon, an ideal base for exploring the shores of the lakes or for casting a fishing line. Further east is Knock, well known for its shrine and apparition but now also known for the International Airport at Charlestown nearby. In the south is Cong, site of the ruined 12th Century Cong Abbey, and where the mountains of Connemara give way to the fertile farmland of east Mayo. Probably the best-known centre in Mayo is the Georgian town of Westport, a popular playground for travelers who wish to get away from the wild western countryside. During the summer the town is very popular with visitors from all over Europe and the United States who return annually to enjoy once again its many charms and also to take in its Art Festival.

Ardmore Country House Hotel

WESTPORT

Having travelled the length and breath of Ireland, I know only too well that wherever you stay can literally make or break your visit and leave an indelible memory. Unfortunately, my first visit to Westport was destroyed by rude receptionists, a stained bed, a dirty room, and bad food and I won't even go into the after effects of that visit but it took six months to recover. Now, if we had only known of the wonderful Ardmore Country House Hotel we could have spared ourselves that disaster.

ARDMORE COUNTRY HOUSE HOTEL

Westport is a busy tourist orientated Town, very pretty, lying on the water, within the shadows of a Great House - the famous 18th C. Westport House belonging to the Altamont family. Just 3 kms from the centre of the town is Pat and Noreen Hoban's Ardmore Country House. Stunningly located overlooking Clew Bay, Ardmore House is in the shadow of Croagh Patrick, enjoying breathtaking sunsets, and is within walking distance of the gates of Westport House. The 13 very large and spacious bedrooms are dramatically and stylishly furnished with luxurious fabrics, wonderful colours, and have all the little extras, one expects nowadays in top hotels, including a turndown service, power shower and good toiletries. Bedroom prices vary depending on whether they are to the front of the house with those spectacular sea views, or have a rural outlook to the rear. Open fires and a tinkling grand piano are what you can expect to enjoy at Ardmore after

you have enjoyed a lovely meal in the Restaurant – it's a grown up place and not suitable for children under 12. Pat Hoban is a fine chef so you can expect to enjoy spanking fresh seafood from Clew Bay, including scallops, and lobster when available. Carnivores are not ignored because prime Irish beef, lamb and wild foul feature too. Organic vegetables and herbs come from local producers along with an extensive selection of Irish farmhouse cheeses. There is an extensive wine list with affordable, as well as fine, wines from all the de rigueur Chateaux for the discerning connoisseur. Pat and Noreen are warm and friendly hosts who will only want to ensure that you enjoy your stay with them and see to your every comfort. Following Ardmore's inclusion in the first edition of my *Little Black Book of Great Places to Stay*, one visitor wrote in the Ardmore guest book "Lucinda O'Sullivan has it just right". Go and find out for yourself.

Owners:	Pat Hoban
Address:	The Quay, Westport, Co. Mayo.
Tel/Fax	098 25994/098 27795
No. Of Rooms	13
Price	
Double/Twin	€170 - €250
Single	€125 - €150
Dinner	Yes
Open	March - December
Credit Cards	Visa MC Amex
Directions.	Leave Westport on R335 Louisburg/Coast road for 3 km, watch for sign.
Email:	ardmorehotel@eircom.net
Web:	www.lucindaosullivan.com/ardmorehousehotel

☐ ⬧ ▰ NET P

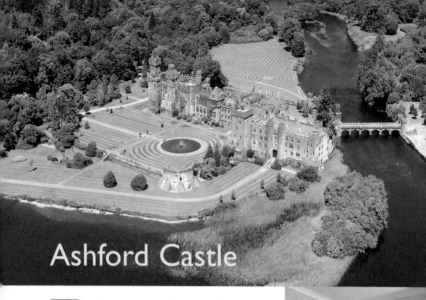

Ashford Castle

The former country home of the Guinness family, Ashford Castle is on 350 acres of the most fantastic grounds, walks, and lakes and is incredibly romantic and evocative. It was founded in the 13th century and through the centuries has had various additions, the most significant being a French Chateau section in 1715 and two Victorian extensions in 1852. The guest book reads like a roll call of the world's most famous people – Princess Grace, Tony Blair, John Ford, John Wayne, Bob Hope, Rod Stewart, Ronald Reagan, Fred Astaire, George V of England...have all graced Ashford Castle...and Pierce Brosnan and his wife Keely chose it for their wedding reception a couple of years ago. However, you don't have to have your name in lights or be mega rich to enjoy Ashford Castle for they also do wonderful special breaks at certain times of the year. There is so much to do within the estate - golf, fishing, clay pigeon shooting, horse riding, Health spa and beauty centre, and the School of Falconry is an incredible experience, not to be missed. Walks through the woods with these birds will bring you straight back to Lancelot and Guinevere. This too is "Quiet Man" country and "Squire Danagher's" house is on the Estate.

The magnificent oak panelled halls lead to a central drawingroom, the social hub of the castle. On our first evening there we dined in The Connaught Room, considered the finest room, with its fairytale Inglenook fireplace and glorious ceiling holding the most exquisite chandelier. If you want a special treat, an experience you will remember, this is it. The sublime 5 or 7 course degustation menu

prepared by Michelin starred Chef Stefan Matz can be had with, or without, wines and you will be waited on with grace and style as you sit romantically facing out to the Lake.

The King George V room is also fabulous with the most luxurious food – Duck Foie Gras Salad poached foie gras with melted figs and sauternes jellies and the most brilliantly delicately wrapped prawns in rosti style; Scallops and Black pudding on creamed potatoes and Seared Monkfish with Connemara Lobster Claw. There is now also an extensive menu for kids with all sorts of games and pictures to keep them occupied. There is something very unique too about the staff – they are all really special "characters" and they do everything possible to make your stay perfect.

Owners:	Niall Rochford (General Manager)
Address:	Ashford Castle, Cong, Co. Mayo.
Tel/Fax	094 9546003/ 094 9546260
No. Of Rooms	83
Price	
Double/Twin	From €217 (Room Only)
Dinner	2 Restaurants
Open	All Year
Credit Cards	All Major Cards
Directions.	In Galway take Castlebar/Headford Road N84. Continue on through Headford and on to the village of Cross. In Cross turn left at the Church for Cong. As you drive into Cong the Castle is on your left
Email:	reservations@ashford.ie
Web:	www.lucindaosullivan.com/ashfordcastle

NET 9h H

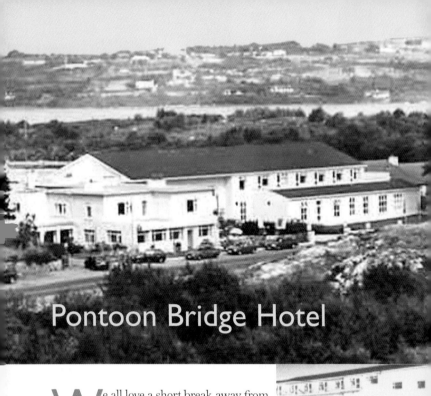

Pontoon Bridge Hotel

We all love a short break away from the family with the girls and I am sure the boys like to head off to for a bit of escapism. There is no doubt but that you return to the fray refreshed and revitalized after a few days.

Pontoon Bridge Hotel is a Mecca for anglers and people who love the water or just want a good time. It has featured on the BBC Holiday programme and on ITV's "Wish You Were Here". The location is absolutely stunning, set on a narrow peninsula right between Lough Conn and Lough Cullin, and with a gallery of mountain ranges, Nephin and Ox as a backdrop. It was bought in 1964 by Brendan and Ann Geary whose children grew up in the family business. Daughter Breeta Geary is now the General Manager, whilst her sister, Mary, apart from being Executive Chef also runs the Cookery School. Other family members are also involved ensuring a personal interest at all times. Apart from the fishing and other outdoor activities, the Pontoon Bridge Hotel run various courses from the aforementioned cookery to landscape painting and fly fishing, all of which make great occasions for that short break. There is also excellent golf available locally. Their wonderful refurbishment programme includes Hot Tub, Sauna and Treatment rooms so that you can be thoroughly pampered. Whatever you do, you can be sure there will be plenty to talk about over

a drink in the evening after dining in any of the hotel's three restaurants – the Twin Lakes for fine dining, the Terrace Bistro and the Waterfront for Bar Food and family ambience, all with splendid views of the lake. Why not check out their mid-week and weekend packages and arrange that break now.

Owners:	The Geary Family Breeta Geary (General Manager)
Address:	Pontoon, Foxford, Co. Mayo.
Tel/Fax	094 9256120/ 094 9256688
No. Of Rooms	39
Price	
Double/Twin	€170 + 12.5% Service
Single	€100 + 12.5% Service
Family	(On request – various sizes)
Dinner	Yes – 3 Restaurants
Open	All Year save 23rd – 26th December
Credit Cards	Visa MC Amex
Directions.	4 miles west of Foxford.
Email:	relax@pontoonbridge.com
Web:	www.lucindaosullivan.com/pontoonbridge

County Offaly

County Offaly, a midland county is bounded by the Shannon River to the northwest and the Slieve Bloom Mountains in south. The old Grand Canal connects the Shannon and the Barrow rivers and passes through Tullamore, the principal county town. The Tullamore name is well known because it was the original home of the distillery that made Tullamore Dew, one of the better brands of Irish Whiskey. West, along the Shannon, is one of the earliest Celtic monasteries and probably the most important one in the country, Clonmacnoise. Continuing south on the River Shannon brings you to Shannonbridge. This is the meeting point of the counties Offaly, Roscommon and Galway, and was once considered to be strategically important, hence the large artillery fortification dating from the Napoleonic era. A visit to County Offaly would not be complete without a visit to Birr with its famous Castle. Home of the Earls of Rosse, the Castle is also the home of the Rosse Telescope built in 1845 by the 3rd Earl and for three quarters of a century it remained the largest telescope in the World. It has been restored and is operational to this day.

"I'm not a social person but I could fall for a duke – they are a great aphrodisiac."
TINA BROWN, Tatler, 1979

& Restaurant

The romantic notion of all the great artists starving in garrets is not entirely true. I watched the famous "living sculpture" artists Gilbert and George tell Sir David Frost on TV that they rose to work very early each morning and had lunch at 11 a.m. sharp! The great French Impressionist, Monet, too had more on his mind than his waterlilies at Giverny if he did not have a jolly good four course lunch at 11.30 a.m., there was hell to pay.

We were in Birr for an Art Exhibition when we discovered what a brilliant town it was for a break and, on top of that, we discovered The Stables. Birr is the most complete Georgian Town in Ireland with uniquely fine squares, malls and streets of splendid houses. Overlooking these wonderful malls and squares is Birr Castle, home of the Earl and Countess of Rosse whose ancestors acquired the Castle and 1277 acres in 1620.

Sweeping up to the private entrance to the Castle is the magnificent Oxmantown Mall with its gracious houses and, this is where you will find Donald and Caroline Boyd's fine townhouse and restaurant – The Stables. The atmosphere is very friendly and welcoming. Off the hall is a very nice drawingroom cum bar area, elegantly furnished, with a blazing fire. So cosy, you could sit there for hours and be elegantly pie eyed.

Curving around the back courtyard, is the restaurant and, believe me, one thing you won't be is hungry when you leave. The décor is subtly rustic, with Francophile undertones; helped on by French style walnut, tapestry upholstered, dining chairs, wrought iron sconces, wagon wheel lights, hunting pictures and yellow brick walls. Lovely local ladies fuss over you making sure you have enough of everything, and the thought of oven roasted venison sausages with a fig and apple chutney, or tiger prawns in filo pastry with sweet jam and chilli, followed perhaps by succulent rack of lamb or honey roast half duckling with an apricot stuffing and Southern Comfort sauce, might get your digestive juices going.

Breakfast is excellent and I have no doubt but that if you stay at The Stables you will return again knowing that you will greeted you as a friend.

 NET

Owners:	Donal & Caroline Boyd,
Address:	6 Oxmantown Mall, Birr, Co. Offaly.
Tel/Fax	0509 20263/0509 21677
No. Of Rooms	6
Price	
Double/Twin	€90
Single	€55
Family	€110
Dinner	Yes – Restaurant
Open	All Year – Closed 23rd/24th/25/26th December
Credit Cards	Visa MC Amex Diners Laser
Directions.	Birr Town Centre opposite Private Gates of Birr Castle
Email:	cboyd@indigo.ie
Web:	www.lucindaosullivan.com/thestables

County Roscommon

Sitting to write about County Roscommon brings back happy memories of many weeks spent boating on the River Shannon, which borders the county to the east. We would rent a cruiser in Jamestown and sail downriver under the bridge at Roosky past Tarmanbarry into beautiful Lough Ree and on down through Athlone et al. We did occasionally stop for a little drop of nourishment in some of the friendly pubs on the way. Roscommon town a pleasant place for a visit has the quaint story about its County Jail, now housing a collection of shops and restaurants. Apparently it was the scene of all the hangings in the county and used to have a woman executioner by the name of Lady Betty. She had her own sentence for murder revoked provided she did the job unremunerated. Strokestown is a well-planned town with an exceptionally wide main street, the idea of some former bigwig who wanted to boast the widest street in Europe. Strokestown Park House, designed by Richard Cassels, with its beautiful gardens and Famine Museum is well worth a visit. Heading west from Strokestown through Tulsk, the home of the legendary Queen Medb, who caused her share of trouble, you come upon Frenchpark, which gave the country its first President, Douglas Hyde, who was also one of the founders of the Gaelic League. Go south a little to Castlerea where it is worth stopping to visit Clonalis, which is the ancestral home of the O'Conor Clan, Kings of Connaught. Clonalis House has a number of interesting paintings charting the family's colourful history at home and abroad. To the north of the county is the town of Boyle on the banks of a river of the same name, an area that has become attractive to many artists, musicians and crafts people and warrants a visit to the Cistercian Boyle Abbey consecrated in 1220.

"Between two evils, I always pick the one I never tried before."
(MAE WEST)

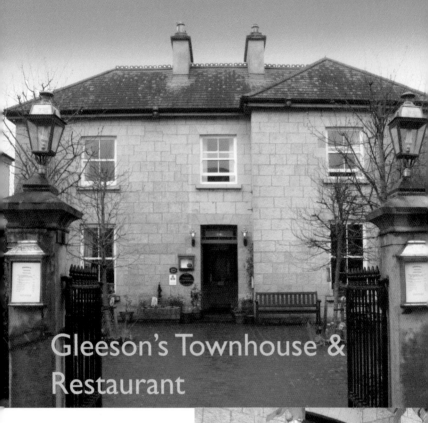

Gleeson's Townhouse & Restaurant

I n the past few years people have come to appreciate the natural unspoiled beauty of Counties Roscommon and Leitrim, which have become destinations for the canny traveller wanting to get away from more obvious tourist haunts. Roscommon Town has plenty to do and see, including the enormous well-preserved Roscommon Castle built by the Normans in 1269, burnt down by the Irish four years later, and rebuilt in 1280. Right in the centre of the town is Gleeson's Townhouse & Restaurant, and this is where you are going to stay when you visit Roscommon, with the very hospitable Eamonn and Mary Gleeson as your hosts. Indeed Eamonn loves to accompany visitors to traditional Irish music "Sessiuns" held locally. That sort of hospitality

and friendliness is what defines Gleeson's and which can be very hard to find in these Celtic Tiger Days. Both former school teachers, the Gleeson's bought the 19th century Manse (a Protestant Minister's House) in a derelict state in 1990, with the intention of opening a small café and B & B.

The comfortable accommodation offers a choice of standard or superior rooms, and one lovely suite overlooking the town's historic square. All rooms have modem connections, direct dial telephones, and satellite television and superior rooms have kingsize beds. Gleeson's is a member of Feile Bia, which demonstrates a commitment to using quality produce in their restaurant, The Manse. Try the Toulouse sausage with bacon and creamy pasta or the crispy duck salad, followed maybe by the roast loin of local lamb, and do pick a decent bottle from the plentiful wine list. Actually, you will never go hungry in Gleeson's because they also have a very good Café which opens for breakfast from 8 a.m. doing delicious home cooked casual food and scrummy cakes and buns all day. Have a look too at the fine stonework and the historic archway at ground level opposite the turf fire stove.

By the way, if you are a golfer or an angler there is a centre for you with cold room, drying room storage and laundry facilities and, they are conveniently next door to a Leisure Centre. They also have a lovely self-catering apartment to let on the waterfront at nearby Lanesboro. The Gleesons seem to have thought of everything to make their guests happy.

Owners:	Eamonn & Mary Gleeson,
Address:	Market Square, Roscommon, Co. Roscommon.
Tel/Fax	0906 626954/0906 627425
No. Of Rooms	19
Price	
Double/Twin	€110 - €130
Single	€55
Family	€140
Dinner	Yes – Restaurant and Cafe
Open	All Year – Closed 25th 26th December
Credit Cards	Visa MC Amex Diners Laser
Directions.	Roscommon Town Centre; Next door to Tourist Office – County Museum.
Email:	info@gleesonstownhouse.com
Web:	www.lucindaosullivan.com/gleesonstownhouse

County Tipperary

Tipperary is the largest of Ireland's inland counties. Situated in the rich fertile lands of the Golden Vale it is also a very wealthy county. Without a doubt, the most outstanding of its many attractions is the Rock of Cashel, rising sharply to over 200 feet and topped by mediaeval walls and buildings. Not far from Cashel is the peaceful town of Cahir on the River Suir with its wonderful Castle dating back to the 13th and the 15th centuries, an Anglo Norman stronghold of the Butlers, the Earls of Ormond. North of Cashel the River Suir passes through the towns of Thurles, not far from Holy Cross Abbey, and is the birthplace of the G.A.A., the ruling body for our National Games. Templemore is like Westpoint on flat feet, being the training headquarters of the Irish Police Force, the Garda Siochana. The area around Nenagh and Lough Derg – Terryglass, Coolbaun, Puckaun -is very popular now with many people having holiday homes near the Lake. Nenagh also boasts a colossal round Castle Keep with walls 20 feet thick and a height of 100 feet topped with 19th century castellations. Clonmel is probably Tipperary's prettiest centre. It was the principal base for Bianconi, the most successful coach company in the 1800's in this country. Clonmel also boasts the 19th century St. Mary's Roman Catholic Church, the 19th century West Gate and the Greek Revival style Wesleyan Church and more. The county has many peaceful and pleasant villages to appeal to visitors such as Bansha, not far from Cahir and backed by the Glen of Aherlow and the Galtee Mountains, or Ballyporeen whose claim to fame is that U.S. President Ronald Regan's grandfather hailed from there.

"An actor's a guy who, if you ain't talking about him,
ain't listening"
(MARLON BRANDO)

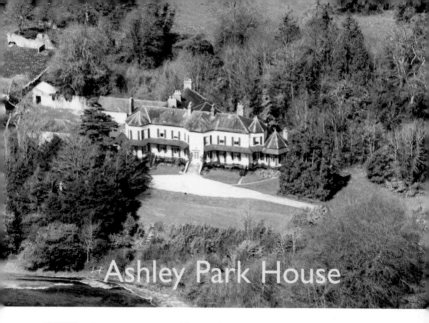

Ashley Park House

The first time I saw Ashley Park House I took a deep intake of breath and thought I had entered the film set of Gone With the Wind or Raintree County. It is a most dramatic and unusual house for this part of the world which would do Savannah proud. An 18th Century house, a white vision with elaborate green painted verandahs, overlooking the sultry Lake Ourne, with hanging weeping trees. Ashley Park House is on 76 acres of beechwood and formal gardens, with strolling peacocks and ancient walled gardens, and is quite spellbinding. Friend Carmel and I had whirled up in my little blue MGF open topped car . Sean Mounsey, the family patriarch complete with cap, who is one of the greatest characters you are ever likely to meet said, "I want you to be happy here Ma'am". I felt like Princess Margaret. Sean took us up to the "Bishop's room" where he had put up a small temporary bed beside the half tester as the house was full and, looking puzzled, said half to himself, "I wasn't expecting two such fine strapping women as yourselves – now if one of you were smaller". Tears streamed down our faces we laughed so much, and as Carmel collapsed over the dressing table in a heap, Sean Mounsey beat a hasty retreat........

Ashley Park House has some of the finest rooms you will ever come across and you can live out all of your Scarlett O'Hara fantasies in this house. The front bedrooms at either end of the house are vast, splendid

and romantic. The house is magnificently furnished with impeccable taste by Sean's daughter Margaret. Relax in the impressive drawingroom with a drink in front of the fire or chill out in the beautiful octagonal Chinese reading room off it. Explore the old walled garden which they are restoring. Dine in the magnificent diningroom. Go to Ashley Park quickly you might not find Rhett Butler but you will find Sean Mounsey and his beautiful daughter Margaret and they are much more interesting altogether. Children are welcome. It is incredible value and an equally incredible experience.

Owners:	P.J. and Margaret Mounsey
Address:	Ashley Park, Nenagh, Co. Tipperary.
Tel/Fax	067 38223/067 38013
No. Of Rooms	5
Price	
Double/Twin	€100 - €110
Single	€50 - €55
Family	€120
Dinner	Yes (Book by 2 p.m.)
Open	All Year
Credit Cards	Visa MC Diners Amex
Directions.	From Nenagh, turn right on the N52 for 3 miles. Ashley Park is the large white house on the opposite side of lake.
Email:	margaret@ashleypark.com
Web:	www.lucindaosullivan.com/ashleyparkhouse

Bailey's of Cashel

I f walls could speak then Bailey's Townhouse would keep a listener enthralled for hours. This very fine house was built in 1703 by The Wesley Family, so is just over 300 years old and has a great history. Dermot and Phil Delaney, who have an excellent pedigree in hospitality, totally revamped and upgraded the house when they bought it a few years ago culminating with the addition this year of a new Leisure Centre with pool, sauna, spa and beauty treatments. Phil's impeccable taste is evident from the moment you set foot on the black and white tiled floor of the gracious Hall with its lovely Farrow & Ball colours. The bedrooms are beautifully furnished and all have data terminals so no matter how far from home you are, you will always be able to stay in contact. Being so centrally located you can just leave the car and walk around historic Cashel returning for a casual lunch or to the drawing room to relax. Breakfast is served in the green dining room overlooking the town. The Cellar Restaurant downstairs, complete with open fire and a well stocked bar, is bistro style with a very wide menu, serving casual food at lunchtime, and lots on offer too for dinner. Phil is a natural cook and a generous one to boot. Their vivacious daughter supervises Service. Bailey's is a superb place to stay when visiting Ireland's most famous monument, the Rock of Cashel. It is also a great spot for a short break – there are lots of golf clubs and pubs and places to see such as the Cashel folk village, Cahir Castle, the picture postcard Swiss Cottage at Cahir and much much more. Oh, if you want a bit of ceoil and rince there are seisiuns in the Bru Boru Heritage Centre from June to September.

Owners:	Phil Delaney
Address:	Main Street, Cashel, Co.
Tipperary.	Tel/Fax 062 61937/062 63957
No. Of Rooms	19
Price	
Double/Twin	€90
Single	€55
Family	€120
Dinner	Yes - Restaurant
Open	All Year
Credit Cards	All Major Cards
Directions.	In Cashel Town Centre
Email:	info@baileys-ireland.com
Web:	

www.lucindaosullivan.com/baileysguesthouse

Bansha Castle

I got a tall order from an English PR agency representing the head of a large Legal Firm. "The Boss" was suffering Hip Hotel Fatigue and looking for something different. He wanted to rent a big Country House where he could entertain his best customers for a week. If it was that simple I would, as they say in Tipperary, be away on a hack, but no, he wanted more and a lot more. He wanted a house where he could self cater and indulge his passion for cooking some nights, and have dinner provided other nights. Still simple you may say but he also wanted a place where he and his friends could hunt, shoot and fish and be within walking distance of the local pub Well you will be delighted to know that I found the perfect retreat at the 18th C. Bansha Castle. As I travelled the road from Cashel to Bansha, it reminded me a little of Beverly Hills without the traffic for it definitely had the mansions, secure Stud Farms and prime beef units. This is 4-wheel drive territory so I knew when I arrived at Bansha Castle that I had backed a winner for Mr. Lawyer. Teresa and John Russell are welcoming hosts and there is a great casual welcoming feel to the whole house. You just know where you can throw your riding jacket on the hall stand, and leave your riding boots at the bottom of the stairs, without fear of reprimand. Teresa will organize the Huntin', Shootin', Fishin' and she can also organize a beautician to come if you want to pamper yourself. The Drawing room is a impressive room with a large full size Pool Table just off. Perfect for someone with a wasted childhood in Pool Halls or for a visiting member of the Mafia. Teresa has organized the House so well that you can rent the whole place and have a private kitchen and dining room at your disposal or she will cook breakfast and dinner for you at times to suit you. If the house is not let then you will have the

opportunity to stay on a B & B basis, and also be able to enjoy a dinner at one of her beautifully laid tables in the large Dining Room where she serves up good unpretentious home cooking. This arrangement also suits people celebrating special occasions, even divorces, and you can bring your own booze.

Owners:	John & Teresa Russell
Address:	Bansha, Co. Tipperary.
Tel/Fax	062 54187/062 54294
No. Of Rooms	6 (for self catering sleeps 12/17)
Price	
Double/Twin	€90
Single	€60
Family	€150 (2 adults + 2 children) The Castle is available for self-catering. It sleeps 12/17. Price on application.
Dinner	Yes – Has to be pre-booked.
Open	All Year
Credit Cards	None
Directions.	Located just outside village of Bansha
Email:	teresa@banshacastle.com
Web:	www.lucindaosullivan.com/banshacastle

Coolbawn Quay Lakeshore Spa

Twenty years ago if you said you were going to a Spa people would have thought you weren't well but, oh boy, once we copped on to the joys of Spas did we ever take to them like ducks to the proverbial waters.   Spas are for you, for me – not just a Leisure Centre where you are "working" watching the kids splash around, or a Health Farm where you go and pay for the joy of starving. Finally there is a place where we can go, be pampered, forget all our worries, have delicious healthy food and just crash out and rejuvenate.

Coolbawn Quay is a unique private village nestling on the shores of Lough Derg, complete with magnificent marina. Understated and elegant, accommodation is in a series of snug village rooms, larger lakeshore suites, or in luxury cottages with French doors to a private decking area. I watched a legendary movie star being interviewed on T.V. and he was asked what was the secret of his long marriage - "separate bathrooms", he replied. At Coolbawn Quay they obviously realise this so, their luxurious cottages have a choice of 2, 3 or 4 bathrooms. Here you will receive full hotel style service and, indeed, you may also dine in your cottage. Alternatively, cottages can also be taken on a self-catering basis.

The Aqua Spa Suite comprises a counter-current pool, sauna and steam room, as well as a relaxation room overlooking the lake. There are all sorts of body wrap treatments, Algimud Body Masks; Deep Sea Black Mud envelopment and facials using the holistic Dr. Hauschka and Rene Guinot products. I had the Algae Seaweed Body wrap which was fabulous leaving my skin exfoliated and feeling like silk. Facials for men are superb too, designed to rejuvenate tired skin.

Owners Jay and Kevin Brophy are also in to food, they once owned a top Dublin restaurant, so you are going to enjoy the very best of delicious fare, using fresh local and organic produce, beautifully prepared by their Chef and served in a the candlelit diningroom. Oh there is a bar too, where you can also imbibe and/or have lunch. Coolbawn is on my agenda for regular de-stress visits.

Get the girls together, you deserve it, or take Himself – maybe he deserves it too – it's the sort of Lough Derg you can both really enjoy!

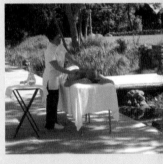

Owners:	Jay & Kevin Brophy
Address:	Coolbawn, Lough Derg, Co. Tipperary.
Tel/Fax	067 28158/067 28162
No. Of Rooms	48
Price	
Double/Twin	From €150
Single	From €105
Family	Children 2-12 years receive 33 % Discount
Dinner	Yes – Restaurant
Open	January to December (Closed Christmas)
Credit Cards	Visa MC Amex Diners Laser
Directions.	From Nenagh N52 to Borrisokane for approx 1Mile, turn left opp AIBP factory, on to Lake Drive Route. Pass through villages of Puckane and Coolbawn. Entrance exactly 2 miles past Coolbawn Village on left.
Email:	info@coolbawnquay.com
Web:	www.lucindaosullivan.com/coolbawnquay

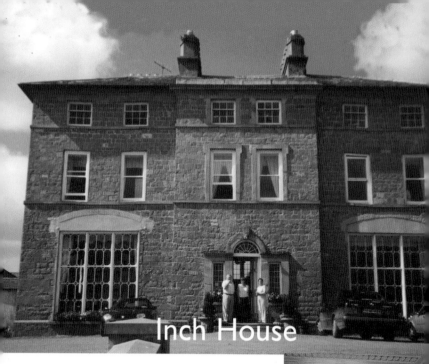

Inch House

Eamonn de Valera was President when I was a child. A very old man at that stage, he was almost blind and was an austere and forbidding figure sitting up in the back of the old State Car wearing a black hat. To me he was a terrifying sight and I didn't like him at all. Well, whatever I thought about the man, he got his own back because when I got married I was in a fairly pressurised job and when we moved into our new house the timing of the move, arranged three months in advance, was down to seconds. The carpet layers were coming first along with the plumbers. De Valera upped and died and the Nation went into mourning. His funeral was on the day of the move, the carpet layers went out in sympathy, whilst the furniture removers from the old house didn't, hence the furniture arrived first and the carpet layers arrived after dark much the worse for the wear ...

INCH HOUSE

John and Nora Egan's Inch House in Thurles sits proud in the middle of lush farmland with a drive up to the stately front door. The first thing you notice about Inch, is the meticulous care given to the pot plants outside the door – perfectly cared for but the second thing I noticed was the portrait of Dev over my bedroom door!   Get John Egan talking about politics and you could have the fun of your life – he is gregarious and brilliant all in one. Nora laughs quietly in the background at the good of it all while she overseas this meticulous well cared for house. Have a drink in the beautiful William Morris papered blue, white and gilt, drawingroom and listen to the local stories. The Restaurant attracts

people from all over the place for the ample well prepared food served by wonderful ladies who will look after you like a mother. The House was the former home of the Ryan family for hundred years– a great Tipperary name- and in fact shortly after I wrote about Inch House I had an email from the Ryans in New Zealand where they have now made there home. Have a look at the stained glass Ryan coat of arms on the staircase the family motto was "Death Before Dishonour". The bedrooms are peaceful and comfortable and you will recline on the finest linen in a Prince Albert bed before coming down to a lavish breakfast in the magnificent diningroom again. It is a beautiful house on wonderful grounds and I can't wait to get back there again.

Owners:	John & Nora Egan
Address:	Thurles, Co. Tipperary.
Tel/Fax	0504 51348/0504 51754
No. Of Rooms	5
Price	
Double/Twin	€110
Single	€65
Dinner	Yes - Restaurant
Open	All Year
Credit Cards	Visa MC Laser
Directions.	From Thurles take Nenagh road for 6 kms past The Ragg. House is on the left.
Email:	inchhse@iol.ie
Web:	www.lucindaosullivan.com/inchhouse

Monaincha House & Health Spa

I am not in the habit of knocking on people's doors and saying "can I come in and have a look" but there was something about the discreet black sign and big gates of Monaincha House and Estate that aroused my curiosity. We were actually heading for Kerry, via Limerick, but I turned the car went back and swept in through the imposing entrance. As we drove up the long driveway through fields of big fat lush cattle and chestnut trees, over a little curvy hump back bridge, up to the pretty entrance and front garden, I knew we were on to something good. We were! Somehow it brought me back to the happy peaceful days I had spent on my aunt's farm, The Grange at Tullow, Co. Carlow, and I thought "wouldn't people love to know about this place".

Monaincha is a beautifully appointed mid 18th Century house, gloriously gracious, and absolutely immaculate. The cool entrance hall is vast, as is the drawingroom and elegant diningroom where breakfast is served. The grounds, gardens and farmland of the Estate are as meticulously maintained by the Moore family as the house and there isn't a place that you wouldn't, as the expression goes, "eat your dinner off the floor". Even those beautiful cows look as if they have been

188

pampered, powdered and manicured. At the time we arrived Carmel and her family were comparative newcomers to Roscrea. They had lived and farmed in Abbeyleix for many years before that but, they too just fell in love with Monaincha House when they saw it, upped sticks, and moved taking on a new challenge.

Since my first visit, Carmel's daughter, Niamh, has opened a Health & Beauty Spa so Monaincha House is the ideal destination if you want a few days to pamper yourself, de-stress or take time out, enjoy beautiful walks through the farmland, whack a ball on the hard tennis court, play a round of golf on the 18 hole golf course which is right next door, then come back and have maybe a Seaweed Detox Wrap or an Indian Head Massage, before you go out to dinner at a local restaurant. Monaincha makes for a very reasonably priced break with lots to visit in the area. Ask Carmel about the great local antiques ...

Owners:	Carmel & Niamh Moore
Address:	Monaincha, Roscrea, Co. Tipperary.
Tel/Fax	0505 23757/0505 23181
No. Of Rooms	3
Price	
Double/Twin	€90
Single	€50
Family	€90 + Under 12's Half Price
Dinner	No
Open	1st April – 31st October (House will open for groups during Winter Months – Health and Beauty Spa open all year)
Credit Cards	Visa MC Laser
Directions.	From Dublin on N7 – On left hand side 3 Km short of Roscrea beside golf course.
Email:	info@monainchahouse.com

Web: www.lucindaosullivan.com/monainchahouse

County Waterford

A walled city of Viking origin, Waterford is the oldest city in Ireland and even today it retains much of its medieval character. It is the home of Waterford Crystal, the world-famous handcrafted, cut glass product. The parameters of the 10th century settlement can be clearly identified in The Viking Triangle. Reginald's Tower is the most historic urban medieval monument in Ireland while the elegant Chamber of Commerce building, the City Hall and the Bishop's Palace are prime examples of beautiful 18th century architecture. Waterford has a long theatrical and musical tradition, which centres on the historic Theatre Royal, which hosts the Waterford International Festival of Light Opera each year. East of the city is the pretty village of Passage East with its ferry service to Ballyhack in Co. Wexford. Stay on the coast road south to the long sandy beach, flanked by woodland, at Woodstown ideal for a quiet stroll or gentle dip in the sea. Go further south to the popular holiday village of Dunmore East which is largely undiscovered by tourists, or go west to the honky tonk family holiday town of Tramore. Further west is the busy commercial town of Dungarvan but swing inland to the beautiful hidden stretch of the River Blackwater around Cappoquin within three miles of Lismore and its ecclesiastical past and most dramatic castle in the country, Lismore Castle, owned by the Duchess of Devonshire. It is a fabulous area and also largely undiscovered by tourists. If you want to learn a few words of the native tongue drive back south to the Irish speaking area of Ring where the language thrives as do other traditions such as music and set dancing.

"Never drink black coffee at lunch, it will keep you awake all afternoon"

(JILLY COOPER attrib)

An Bohreen

J im and Ann Mulligan built their perfect Architectural style house
overlooking Dungarvan Bay with guests in mind.   Dublin born Jim
spent most of his life in "Frasier" territory – Seattle - whilst delightful
Ann is American - the most fabulous cook, with a penchant for French
food. The heart of the house is the split-level airy sitting cum dining
area with splendid views right down over the Gaeltacht area of Ring,
Dungarvan Bay and its oyster beds whilst pretty bedrooms, have surreal
views of the brooding Comeragh Mountains.

Dinner may be seafood followed by West Waterford Lamb, Loin of
Pork or Helvick (wild) Salmon – Ann likes to know your choice of main
course in advance and will also tempt with delicious puddings – there
is no limit to this woman's talent.   Almond and Pine nut Tart - "would
you like it with strawberries. ...and perhaps a drizzle of blueberry
reduction mixed with Rumtopf?" Would you what?

At breakfast perfection starts again with pretty dishes of orange
butter, hot scones and homemade preserves. Freshly squeezed orange
juice too "if you don't like the bits, I can strain it", plus a beautiful bowl
of elegantly sliced fruit. Apart from the Full Irish there may be
pancakes with caramelised apple; porridge with Irish Mist; scrambled
egg with smoked salmon or cheese- "American style – firm or Irish style
- soft"!

I watched Jim talk to American visitors and admired his
enthusiasm for his native country.   Having directed guests to various
potteries and booked their next stay, he said "If you have time", I will
take you up to see the Fairy Bush. Past the Famine Graveyard, on over

the cattle grid in to Mahon Falls Park, past cheeky curly horned sheep hanging on to the side of cliffs, wild rugged and absolutely magnificent. The Fairy Bush is adorned with bits of ribbon and mementos but, the idea is, you drive down the hill, stop at the Fairy Bush, and 'lo and behold your car starts to reverse back up the hill on its own ... and it does ... try it. You'll be rushing out to buy Faith of our Fathers all over again! It is a very undiscovered part of Ireland and a great base for walkers, foodies or golfers. They will package a golf holiday for you ... and the weekly nearby Seisuns, Jim tells us, are so fabulous they "make the hair stand on the back of your neck".

Owners:	Jim and Ann Mulligan, Killineen West, Dungarvan, Co. Waterford.
Tel/Fax	051 291010/051291011
No. of Rooms	4
Price	
Double/Twin	€75-80
Single	€50-55
Dinner	Yes
Open	Mid March – End October
Credit Cards	Visa MC
Directions	From Waterford - 3.1 miles from "Resume Speed" sign turn right at sign. From Dungarvan: 5 miles on Waterford Road turn left at "Slow Lane Ends" sign.
Email:	mulligans@anbohreen.com
Web:	www.lucindaosullivan.com/anbohreen

NET P

Athenaeum House Hotel

"I watched the Tall Ships sail gracefully by from here – it was absolute heaven", I said to friend Miranda. We were sipping champagne on the terrace of Zak's Restaurant at the Athenaeum, a chic new boutique hotel on ten acres, with views down over the river Suir and marina at Waterford Harbour. The best of modern classical taste and design has gone into the Athenaeum – not a frill in sight - just clean lines and stunning colours. From the Grand Piano in the elegant anti-room to the beautiful side chairs in the hall, the Athenaeum is different. Cardinal purple carpets lead down to the bedrooms, which are understated and elegant, but with funky chairs, flat screen television, modem connections, fridge, and anything else today's discerning traveller might want.

Stan Power and his wife Mailo cannot do enough for you. Stan is so cool, professional and helpful, I would imagine if he had been captaining the Titanic it would have made it to New York. Mailo is an Interior Decorator and is responsible for the slick beautiful cool décor with its clean architectural lines and modern classical atmosphere, which has been wowing the who's who of Irish society, who have been beating a path to their door.

Zak's Restaurant, which is one of the most attractive dining rooms in the country, runs across the back of the hotel. Long and conservatory style, with those great views, you won't however be too distracted from what is on your plate, which is just delicious and also very well priced. Do have dinner and think Tartare of diced salmon,

onion, capers and chives, wrapped in a saffron cream and salmon pearls, or lightly sautéed foie gras on brioche served with duck liver pate with caramelised apple chutney followed, maybe, by the pinkest rack of lamb with aubergine Provencal or Dover Sole. You can look forward to a lovely breakfast too – try their muesli complete with cardamom seeds – they could sell that by the stone weight and make a fortune.

This lovely boutique Hotel on the banks of the River Suir is a real find.

NET H P

Owners:	Stan & Mailo Power
Address:	Christendom, Ferrybank Waterford,
Tel/Fax	051 833999/051 833977
No. of Rooms	29
Price	
Double/Twin	€120/€120
Single	
Family	
Dinner	Yes – Restaurant
Open	All Year
Credit Cards	Visa MC Amex Laser
Directions	From roundabout at Railway Station take N25 in direction of Wexford. After traffic lights take first right on to Abbey Road, then first right after hump back bridge.
Email:	info@athenaeumhousehotel.com
Web:	www.lucindaosullivan.com/athenaeum

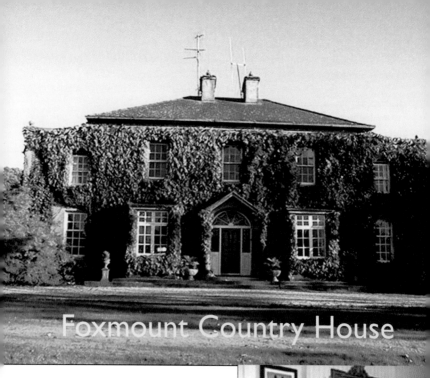

Foxmount Country House

Our French visitors, Michelle and Zandra, had expressed a definite interest in visiting the Waterford Glass Factory so, the decision was taken, to drive down and overnight in Waterford. We drove down through Wicklow, the Garden of Ireland, and Wexford and duly did the tour of the Waterford Glass Factory. Living in Paris, the idea of an Irish farm appealed and I had one up my sleeve. They took a sharp intake of breath when the ivy clad Foxmount House came into view. "Oh, this is beautiful", they exclaimed of its impeccably kept lawns, glorious flower beds and gravel paths, that looked as if they had been fine combed. Inside, too, they were delighted with a blazing fire in the drawingroom, as they admired the family silver, antiques, and general good taste of Margaret and David Kent who, with their son and daughter, run this lovely house and dairy farm to perfection. Michelle and Zandra were anxious to explore the farm so David took them under his wing and showed them around. Some time later I looked out my lovely bedroom window and was surprised to see the pair of them belting a ball back and forth out on the tennis court, but what struck me most when I gazed out the window was being able to see into Margaret Kent's kitchen where perched on the windowsill was a perfectly arranged bowl of soft and dewy pink roses. For me, that said it all. Foxmount House is perfection, from the sign on the main road, right through to the hidden sections of the kitchen. Breakfast was beautifully presented with little bowls of floating flowers and leaves. Delicious breads and scones with homemade preserves sit on beautiful plates followed by a delicious cooked breakfast. I couldn't resist picking up all of the plates and looking underneath to see who made them! One of the brilliant things about Foxmount too is its location. It is a farm on the edge of Waterford City so you are in to the centre by taxi or car in literally ten minutes, yet you have the joy of being close to the sea, you are on the road down to the little ferry in picturesque Passage East and very close to any number of golf courses.

Owners:	David & Margaret Kent
Address:	Passage East Road, Waterford.
Tel/Fax	051 874308/051 854906
No. Of Rooms	5
Price	
Double/Twin	€110
Single	€65
Dinner	No
Open	Mid March – 1st November
Credit Cards	No
Directions.	Take Dunmore East Road from Waterford City, then take Passage East Road for one mile. Sign on right for house.
Email:	info@foxmountcountryhouse.com
Web:	www.lucindaosullivan.com/foxmount

Glasha Farmhouse

You know that great Irish welcome that we all boast about and very often don't find - well you can be sure of it at Olive and Paddy O'Gorman's lovely Glasha Farmhouse set in the beautiful Nire Valley. It is a large white house impeccably maintained and, as you drive in and get out of your car with your bags and baggage, you are suddenly swept up in the enthusiastic warm welcome that Olive bestows on everyone - no wonder she was the first B & B to win the Failte Ireland Warm Welcome Award. Before you know where you are, you are ensconced on comfortable sofas being plied with tea and apple tart while Olive talks a dime a dozen. Paddy is delightful, a gentle smiling farmer, who knows and is proud of what Olive has achieved and her enthusiasm for visitors and tourists. Olive has thought of everything for the very comfortable bedrooms, with all sorts of extras like electric blankets, hairdryers and nick nacks often lacking in good hotels - and some rooms have Jacuzzi baths. The Nire Valley is very popular with walkers and anglers but you can drive around like me if you wish!! These are the real hidden places of Ireland very often not found by Tourists as they beat a track for the West. The river Nire runs beside Glasha and fishing permits are available locally. Have a delicious dinner - maybe Rack of Comeragh Lamb or Poached Monkfish, and, if you are good, Olive and Paddy will show you the back gate, which slips out onto a little windy road where at the foot of the hill is one of the dinkiest old pubs I have ever been in. It is like something out of a movie - absolutely wonderful and a perfect way to end the day before strolling back up to Glasha for a wonderfully peaceful sleep in the stillness of Ballymacarbry. Come down next morning and you are in for one of the best breakfasts in Ireland - what a spread Olive puts out - you will have the camera out - it is one of the best I have ever seen.

Houses like Glasha are the real hidden places of Ireland very often not found by the tourist. You are in for a treat.

Owners:	Paddy & Olive O'Gorman
Address:	Glasha, Ballymacarbry, via Clonmel, Co. Waterford.
Tel/Fax	052 36108/052 36108
No. Of Rooms	8
Price	
Double/Twin	€100
Single	€60
Family	€120
Dinner	Yes
Open	All Year except Christmas
Credit Cards	Visa MC
Directions.	Signposted on Clonmel to Dungarvan Road
Email:	glasha@eircom.net
Web:	www.lucindaosullivan.com/glasha

NET P

Richmond Country House

Richmond House is the real thing – no faux Georgian facades here - everything about it is real, classy, elegant and understated. The house, built in 1704 by the Earl of Cork and Burlington, looms tall and stately, gazing serenely out over the fields and private parkland, in the heart of the Blackwater Valley. It has been the Deevy family home for forty years or so as Jean Deevy and her late husband raised their six children there. To aid the restoration and upkeep of such a large house, Jean started out simply doing Bed & Breakfast when en-suites were "en heard of". She provided very well cooked homely food, introducing to her repertoire the "rage of the time" the old prawn cocktail – always being a winner. Times move on and Richmond House is now a place to be reckoned with for Jean's son, Paul, is a very fine Chef, having trained in the Hotel Industry, moving on then to Switzerland, before returning to take up the reins at Richmond House along with his wife, Claire. The bedrooms are gracious and spacious, furnished with antiques, and so comfortable you just want to snuggle in there and not move out. Have a drink in the old conservatory or in the butter yellow drawingroom, meet the people, who will be salivating at the thought of Paul Deevy's innovative but classically French oriented food. Think Fresh Chorizo risotto with steamed mussels and a light butter sauce followed by local fillet of lamb with tapenade, sundried tomatoes and a rosemary jus ... have the Crinnaugtaun apple juice at breakfast ... it helps the hangover.

Richmond House is a perfect place to stay for visiting West Waterford including the beautiful Lismore Castle, which is literally just down the road. The whole area is absolutely beautiful with lots of interesting inhabitants and places to visit, and you will be at the heart of it in Richmond House.

Owners:	Paul & Claire Deevy
Address:	Cappoquin, Co. Waterford.
Tel/Fax	058 54278/058 54988
No. Of Rooms	9
Price	
Double/Twin	€150
Single	€75
Dinner	Yes - Restaurant
Open	January 23rd – December 23rd
Credit Cards	All Major Cards
Directions.	Take Waterford Road from Cappoquin, Richmond House is on the right.
Email:	info@richmondhouse.net
Web:	www.lucindaosullivan.com/richmond

Waterford Castle
Hotel & Golf Club

Somebody said to me one time "Waterford Castle is decorated just the way a Castle should be". Rich and regal with lavish antiques, ornate plaster ceilings, and all the elegance of the original features preserved, it is just perfect. From the moment you pass through the carved granite arch and the studded oak door into the amazing hall, dominated by a beautiful Elizabethan stone cavernous fireplace and magnificent tapestries from generations of yore, you are in another world. You will notice on the chimneybreast, raised proud from the stone like some giant ornate jewel, the carved Fitzgerald coat of arms. Likewise the crested carpet on the floor, for Waterford Castle, built in the 15th Century, and the Norman Keep before that, was in the hands of the Fitzgerald family for 800 years. Fabulously located on its own private 310 acre island estate on the River Suir, yet just 2 miles out of the hustle and bustle of Waterford City, the Castle is surrounded by woodlands and an 18 hole Championship Golf Course. How do we get to the island, I can hear you ask? You just nip out the Dunmore East Road, turn left at the sign and head down to the private ferry which transports you across the little channel into another world of luxurious retreat, sanctuary and seclusion. Over a thousand years ago the first inhabitants cut a rough track to their secure settlement but this is now a tree lined driveway, lush, with ever changing colours and ahead stands the stunning Castle, picturesque and enchanting.

The splendid guest rooms and suites are bright and airy with magnificent views of the surrounding estate and golf course. Guests get the feeling, for this is the way that they are received, that they are residents rather than "hotel guests". Dinner in the Munster Dining Room with its original oak panelled walls and ornate ceilings is a memorable occasion. The

Chef will tempt you with perhaps Kebabs of Dublin Bay Prawns with Roast Garlic, Basil and Cherry tomatoes followed by such delicious goodies as Moroccan Spiced Fillet of Aged Beef with cous cous salad and a Pepper Salsa Verde. Go and be a part of this Fairy Tale lifestyle.

Owners:	Gillian Butler (General Manager)
Address:	The Island, Ballinakill, Waterford.
Tel/Fax	051 878203/051 879316
No. Of Rooms	19
Price	
Double/Twin	From €234
Family	On request
Dinner	Yes - Restaurant
Open	Open All Year save 24th 25th 26th Dec and 3rd Jan – 5th Feb.
Credit Cards	All Major Cards
Directions.	Look out for sign to left off Dunmore East Road.
Email:	info@waterfordcastle.com
Web:	

www.lucindaosullivan.com/waterfordcastle

18h NET H P

County Wexford

The Vikings have a lot to answer for when you think of the number of Irish Towns they have founded. Wexford in the southeast, the sunniest part of the Country, is another example of their handiwork. It's very narrow streets are now teeming with thriving shops and businesses and, along the quayside, on the Slaney estuary stands a statue to Commadore John Barry, the Wexford man who founded the U.S. Navy during their War of Independence. This lively town is host to the ever popular and important Wexford Opera Festival every year. South of the town, almost on the extreme southeast corner of the country is Rosslare Strand with its magnificent beach and two 18 hole golf courses. Rosslare Strand is very popular with Irish people but very often missed by tourists who disembark from the ferry at Rosslare

Harbour and drive madly out of the area. Going north the county has many towns with historic connections and none more so than Enniscorthy. Enjoy its period atmosphere and its connection with the 1798 Rebellion with its backdrop of Vinegar Hill site of a famous battle of the same name. Also worth seeing is the Pugin designed St. Aidan's Cathedral. Of more recent interest are the sandy beaches at Curracloe where Steven Speilberg shot those realistic battle scenes for his movie "Saving Private Ryan". In the south west of the county, on the banks of the Barrow Estuary in the quaint village of Arthurstown close to Dunbrody Abbey and less than a mile from Ballyhack from whence the ferry runs to Passage East in County Waterford.

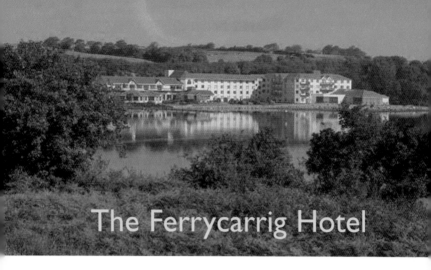

The Ferrycarrig Hotel

The Ferrycarrig Hotel is set low down by the River Slaney Estuary just outside Wexford town and is a fantastic place to stay for all ages, families, couples, just everyone, for it is lively and friendly, providing excellent food and all facilities required for the perfect fun relaxing break. I first visited the Ferrycarrig many years ago before the hotel was converted into the smart place it is today. I got off to a rocky start because, of course, I was travelling anonymously and I described their then corridors as Prague 1963 and made reference to the little lift which dropped six inches before it took off upwards. I have to say they took it magnificently and, with a considerable sense of humour, invited me back some months later to officially declare open the new lift! None of those idiosyncrasies will be found now in the stylish new Ferrycarrig, which has been completely renovated - in fact I rather miss the little lift.

The bedrooms are large and spacious with cool modern East Coast American style décor - very smart - and some have balconies. It is absolute bliss just to sit in the stillness of your room and look out over the water - that for me is always important. The most recent change at the Ferrycarrig is their lovely new restaurant Reeds, which is cool, calm and smart, in neutral shades with wonderful views out over the water. The food is excellent and of course being in the sunny south east there is plenty of delicious seafood - think of all those lovely Kilmore Quay scallops and Duncannon monkfish having started perhaps with Prosciutto and

Turkish figs or Kilmore crabmeat...and then puds.... wow   It is a very interesting hotel to walk around from the big Moroccan style residents' lounge to the tucked away little areas off the bar. There is an excellent leisure centre and a very well supervised pool and it is very close to the Heritage Park and all the facilities of Wexford Town, so there is no doubt but that you will enjoy your stay at the Ferrycarrig.

Owners:	The Griffin Hotel Group
Address:	Ferrycarrig Bridge, Wexford.
Tel/Fax	053 20999/053 20982
No. Of Rooms	102
Price	
Double/Twin	From €130
Single	From €100
Family	From €219
Dinner	Yes - Restaurant
Open	All Year
Credit Cards	Visa MC Diners Amex
Directions.	On N11 - Two miles north of Wexford Town.

Email:	ferrycarrig@ferrycarrighotel.com
Web:	www.lucindaosullivan.com/ferrycarrig

        NET P

Glendine Country House

ARTHURSTOWN AND BALLYHACK

From whichever side you approach Arthurstown and Ballyhack on the Hook peninsula, there is a positive feel of never neverland. Coming from either Dublin or from Rosslare, the Duncannon roundabout outside Wexford is where you change worlds. Sit back and head straight out towards Ballyhack, trundling through hedgerows, along miles of straight road downward towards the sea, taking you little by little back into history to this totally undeveloped area. From the Waterford side, you take the car ferry at Passage East,it only takes a few minutes but the scene is set and as you approach Ballyhack and its 16th Century Castle you are almost exhilarated. Have a pint of the black stuff in the local pub you deserve it after that five minute voyage!

GLENDINE COUNTRY HOUSE.

Tom and Ann Crosbie's fine Georgian Country House sits on 50 acres of beautifully landscaped gardens and paddocks, which hold their Highland cows, Jacob sheep (the ones with the curly horns) and deer. A Dower house to the Dunbrody Estate it was first occupied by the Chichester family and later by land agents until one of them absconded with the Nursery Nurse causing a great scandal. Glendine retains many of its original 1830 features, and, overlooking the Barrow Estuary, all of the rooms are stylishly beautiful and all have magnificent sea views. Beautifully decorated, using soft historic Farrow & Ball colours, the original large en suite bedrooms have Victorian beds, pitch pine floors, crisp cotton sheets, original wooden shutters. In the past year a wing of new bedrooms has been added and these too are absolutely beautiful, large and spacious. All rooms have T.V. and all mod cons. The lovely yellow drawingroom with fine fireplace, antiques and works of art, is comfortable and welcoming.

Breakfasts are hearty and wholesome, where possible using organic produce. Help yourself to a fine range of fresh fruits, cereals, porridge, yoghurts and juices followed by delicious cooked breakfast with lashings of wholemeal toast or homemade brown bread. Two cosy 4**** Self catering cottages are available in the courtyard, converted from the original 1830 stone buildings, and these sleep five people comfortably. Dinner is not available but soup and

open brown bread sandwiches are happily provided at all times. There are very nice Restaurants close by and excellent pub grub. Glendine has a wine licence but you can bring your own. This is a gorgeous house, Tosh and Annie are charming hosts, and you couldn't find a finer place to stay.

Owners:	Tom & Ann Crosbie
Address:	Arthurstown, Co. Wexford
Tel/Fax	051 389500/051 389677
No. Of Rooms	6
Price	
Double/Twin	€80 - €100
Single	€55 (supp €15 July + August)
Family	€120 (2 Ad + 1 Ch) €140 (2 Ad + 2 Ch)
Dinner	No (Light Suppers Only)
Open	All Year except Christmas
Credit Cards	Visa MC Diners
Directions.	From New Ross turn right at Brandon House Hotel. Pass JFK Arboretum, Arthurstown is signposted.
Email:	glendinehouse@eircom.net
Web:	www.lucindaosullivan.com

Kelly's Resort Hotel & Sea Spa

Since 1895 four successive generations of the Kelly family have each added their own stamp to Kelly's Resort Hotel. Bill Kelly and his wife, Isabelle, have, in turn, enlarged and added a whole new cool modern dimension in the last few years culminating in the addition of the fabulous new SeaSpa incorporating eleven treatment rooms, seawater vitality pool, rainforest shower, rock sauna laconium steam room, mud chamber and seaweed bath, which has been their biggest project ever.

Being right on the beach there is that upmarket sandy resort ethos and atmosphere, for, as soon as you swish up and park, you will see people strolling around in bathrobes between Spa, Leisure, Beauty Centre, Hairdresser or Hot Tub – it is just switch off time. I know people who drive down to Kelly's, park their car, and don't move it again until they are leaving Rosslare Strand. Why would they, everything one could possibly want is encompassed within the Hotel. When one mentions Kelly's Hotel, people generally say – "Oh, the food is fabulous, and one eats so much". That's true. It's like a cruise ship, non-stop wonderful food all included in your rate.

Breakfast and lunch are available buffet style in the Ivy Room or with formal service in the gorgeous Beaches Restaurant, which had over a €1m spent on it alone not so long ago. Likewise with lunch, not forgetting afternoon tea and all day availability of free coffee. In the evening people gather for drinks before dinner - which is always superb – oysters, foie gras terrine, game, fish, just as much of anything you could want and Kelly's import their wine direct from France, where Isabelle's family are in the wine business in the Chateauneuf-du-Pape region, resulting in excellent very well priced wines. Dancing follows dinner so join in the fun. Bedrooms are lovely – some with doors

opening out onto your own mini terrace or else have balconies. There is also the La Marine Restaurant (not included in the "all in" rate) and Bar which is popular with visitors to Rosslare. Kelly's Irish Art Collection is famed and in this regard it is opportune to mention that throughout the year there are different breaks revolving around Art, Cookery, Wine, Antiques, Gardening, Ballroom Dancing and of course golf. Kelly's mainly operates on an all-inclusive package, anything from two days to a week and, for what is included, it is superb value. Sometimes, midweek only, they do a room and breakfast rate if that is what you want and you can dine in either Beaches or La Marine. I don't think it is possible for Bill & Isabelle to carry out any further improvements!

Owner:	Bill Kelly
Address:	Rosslare Strand, Co. Wexford.
Tel/Fax	053 32114 / 053 32222
No. Of Rooms	118
Price	
Double/Twin	€170 + 10% Service Charge
Single	€ 95 + 10% Service Charge
Family	On request
	All inclusive rates from €280pps + 10% (for 2 days upwards)
Dinner	Yes – 2 Restaurants
Open	17th February to 10th December
Credit Cards	Visa MC Amex
Directions.	On Rosslare Strand
Email:	kellyhot@iol.ie
Web:	www.lucindaosullivan.com/kellyshotel

NET H P

Monart Luxury Destination Spa

Many people were horrified to hear recently that in England little girls were being taken to Spas to have beauty treatments and were so pampered and powdered that they then didn't want to take part in normal childhood games in case they would destroy their manicures or pedicures!

This certainly won't happen at Monart, the fabulous new Spa at Enniscorthy, for this is a serious stand alone Destination Spa built strictly for adults only The original and beautiful 18th Century Monart House is restored and now acts as a gateway to a stunning 21st Century Spa experience designed from arrival to departure with the emphasis on the 3 R's, not the ones you learned at school, but Rest, Relaxation and Renewal.

Built to the highest international specifications, and located within a 120 acre private estate, Monart's 70 luxury bedrooms and suites have been designed to provide soothing yet sumptuous interiors allowing guests to get up close and personal with the surrounding magnificent mature woodland, for we all know the restorative powers of nature. The gardens have been designed by Chelsea Flower Show Gold Medal Winner, Mary Reynolds.

Monart offers the most comprehensive and leading edge ranges of Spa facilities and treatments and has an exclusive partnership with the top American Spa product line Pevonia Botanica. In its vast 2400 square meters, the Spa area contains 14 neutral gender treatment rooms, sanarium, outdoor Swedish log sauna with ice shower grotto, caldarium, aroma cave, salt grotto, traditional Hamam, mud chamber, hydrotherapy pools to name but a few. So think along the lines of luxuriating in a Full Body Detox Seaweed Thalasso Wrap for the poor

old body, and achieving inch loss as well. Another good one is the Green Coffee Body wrap for breakdown of cellulite and fat, which also helps transform fat into energy. The Elasto-firm facemask treatment, cited as a non-surgical face-lift, is also popular.

There are two dining options at Monart offering excellent contemporary food along with specifically tailored "healthy" menus to complement health and wellness programmes. The first option is the fine dining, reservations only, restaurant and there is also a more casual daytime café restaurant for residential and day Spa clients, where the emphasis is very much on fresh, locally sourced, traditionally healthy fare.

With the new roads it is a mere 90 minutes from Dublin Airport.

Owners:	The Griffin Group
	Mark Browne (General Manager)
Address:	The Still, Enniscorthy, Co. Wexford.
Tel/Fax	054 38999
No. Of Rooms	70
Price	
Double/Twin	From €430 including unlimited access to Spa area
Single	
Dinner	Yes
Open	All Year
Credit Cards	All Major Cards
Directions.	Access from all major routes (N11;N30;N25). To Enniscorthy Town; Follow signposts to Monart.
Email:	info@monart.ie
Web:	www.lucindaosullivan.com/monart

□ 🚜 🔪 💳 NET P H

County Wicklow

Truly the Garden of Ireland, County Wicklow, is rich in mountains, valleys, gorse, heather, and bracken, and as any hiker, cyclist and motorist will undoubtedly agree, it more than deserves its title. Less than an hour's drive from Dublin City, the county quickly portrays the two dominant traditions in Irish history, Glendalough with its Monastic background and the magnificent Anglo Irish Powerscourt Estate at Enniskerry. Glendalough set in a remote valley is a mediaeval Monastic site with its period cemetery, round tower, remains of a monastic chapel and its two lakes, is a very popular haunt for tourists. The area is surrounded by a number of pleasant welcoming villages, Kiltegan, Knockree, Roundwood, Laragh, Rathdrum and, of course, Avoca whose name was made famous by the poet Thomas Moore, and the peaceful village of Aughrim. Enniskerry in the foothills of the Wicklow Mountains is a very popular summer weekend destination for tourists, who trudge uphill from buses to the Powerscourt Estate and its beautiful gardens. Powerscourt also boasts two 18-hole golf courses. The impressive Powerscourt House designed by Richard Cassels was destroyed by fire in 1974, it has now been restored to house a number of shops and a restaurant. The famous Powerscourt Waterfall is almost three miles away from the main house but is still within the Estate's extensive grounds. On the coast to the south is Greystones a pretty somnambulant town where many of the inhabitants commute to Dublin daily and is close to the town in Ireland with the longest name, Newtownmountkennedy. Further south is Wicklow town, which enjoys a fine setting on the coast, and proudly proclaims its restored historic jail. On south past the beautiful sandy beach at Brittas Bay brings you to Arklow town a chiefly commercial centre well known as a boat building and fishing port and immortalized by Van Morrison in his "Streets of Arklow".

"It takes a lot of experience for a girl to kiss like a beginner."
(LADIES HOME JOURNAL, 1948)

Barraderry Country House

What do you do if you own a beautiful large country house and your children have grown up and left the nest? Open it up to visitors so that they may have the pleasure of staying not only in a lovely Country House, but you also have a new interest, and get to meet people from all over the world. This is precisely what Olive and John Hobson did with their lovely Barraderry House in County Wicklow, the Garden of Ireland when they became "empty nesters".

Barraderry House is situated at Kiltegan in the magnificent lush heartlands of Wicklow, Carlow and Kildare and, as such, it makes a fantastic base from which to work outwards through any of these counties. It also has very quick access to Dublin on the N81, linking then to the M50 for Dublin Airport. There is so much to do and see in this fabulous area, which is spectacular in itself. Northwards you are but a short distance from Glendalough (Valley of the Two Lakes) a magical setting for one of the best-preserved monastic sites in the country. There is an unbelievable feel of peace and tranquillity at Glendalough and I always feel, as I leave, that a few hours there is not enough. Head southwest from Kiltegan and you reach Kilkenny City and southeast will bring you to Wexford. So, this whole area is a sheer joy, whether you are a walker or a driver. There are six Golf Courses within thirty minutes drive, as well as equestrian centres and several hunts. Barraderry too is ideal for racing at Punchestown, the Curragh, Naas, or for visiting The National Stud.

The house is delightful, 17th century Georgian, imposing but friendly. Once you sweep up to the front door and enter the fine hall you get that immediate feeling of peace and tranquillity. The bedrooms are big and serene, furnished with family antiques. You are away from the world but you also have the facilities of TV in the bedroom, perfect ensuites, and there is also internet access available. Stroll or sit in the lovely gardens under trees that have been there for generations, or relax in the sittingroom. It is so peaceful you will be assured of a great night's sleep before you come down to a wonderful breakfast and set off exploring the countryside again.

Barraderry could not be better.

Owners:	Olive & John Hobson.
Address:	Barraderry, Kiltegan, Co. Wicklow.
Tel/Fax	059 64 73209/05964 73209
No. Of Rooms	4
Price	
Double/Twin	€90
Single	€50
Dinner	No
Open	15th January – 15th December
Credit Cards	Visa MC
Directions.	From Dublin. N81 to Baltinglass. Left R747 for Kiltegan. Entrance on right before village.
Email:	jo.hobson@oceanfree.net
Web:	www.lucindaosullivan.com/barraderry

Houses in alphabetical order

Slow down

Enjoying Ireland is not about tearing down a motorway at 90 miles an hour, for doing it that way you will miss the whole ethos of the country. Tourists planning their trip in advance from America and other distant places tend to look at our little green, bear shaped, island in the Atlantic on the edge of Europe and think "we'll see it all in 3 days" – believe me you won't have even "done" West Cork properly in that time. You may have seen the views but you won't have experienced anything except a sore backside from sitting in the driving seat!

Take time out, get to know your hosts, it makes such a difference. They can give you all the local lore and recommendations. Go down to the local pub – you won't be long on your own – because the Irish love to talk. Every time I arrive at a destination, my first stop is the nearest hairdressers, which absolutely delights Brendan, for he then has an hour to find the best pub and in no time at all, the locals will have found out his seed, breed and generation, and he will have been rewarded with the best local information.

In the immortal words of Simon and Garfunkel - "Slow Down You Move to Fast..."

Lucinda

Unless otherwise stated room prices include breakfast. Apart from Hotels we suggest that you make arrangements for dinner on the night of your arrival at the same time as you book your accommodation as most houses would like 24 hours notice.

FLEUR DU CAP

Wines inspired by nature.

A WORLD OF TASTES JUST WAITING TO BE DISCOVERED

Febvre is a family owned business, built on a commitment to provide discerning Irish palates with a selection of carefully chosen wines from around the world.

We bring you these wines through our close links with grower-producers, both large and small, who share our desire to uphold the traditions of quality and good taste for which family owned vineyards are renowned.

FEBVRE

Highfield House, Burton Hall Road, Sandyford Industrial Estate, Dublin 18.
Tel: (01) 216 1400   Fax: (01) 295 9036   Email: info@febvre.ie